Lean Years, Happy Years

Lean Years,
Happy Years

ANGELO M. PELLEGRINI

Drawings by Drew Elicker

MADRONA PUBLISHERS • *Seattle* • *1983*

Published by
Madrona Publishers, Inc.
P. O. Box 22667
Seattle, Washington 98122

10 9 8 7 6 5 4 3 2 1

Library of Congress Cataloging in Publication Data

Pellegrini, Angelo M.
Lean years, happy years.

Contents: The lean and happy years ahead — The garden — The kitchen — [etc.]
1. Food—Addresses, essays, lectures. 2. Gardening—Addresses, essays, lectures. 3. Cookery—Addresses, essays, lectures. 4. Wine and wine making—Addresses, essays, lectures. I. Title.

TX355.5.P44 1983   641.3   83-13578
ISBN 0-914842-98-6

The form and substance of this book were conceived when I was participating in teaching an interdisciplinary course on ecological scarcity at the Evergreen State College. My colleagues on that teaching team were Dean York Wong and Professors Beryl Crowe and Larry Eicksteadt. To them, congenial and inspiring, and to the college and its president, Dan Evans, I dedicate this labor of love and contentment.

Contents

Lean Years, Happy Years

The Lean and Happy Days Ahead

WHEN I was a peasant boy in Italy, there was an imperative I heard daily and daily dreaded hearing. It was, in substance, a grace before dinner and preceded by the cruciform gesture traditional in Catholic homes: *Bisogna fare a miccino col formaggio perché ce n'è poco.* We must take the cheese in tiny bites because we have so little of it. Imagine a family of seven sitting down to lunch in early summer. On the table are green onions, a large round loaf of coarse bread, and a small wedge of Parmesan cheese. Mother presses the loaf against her breast, holds it firmly there with her left hand, and drawing the knife through it with her right, slices it. I remember observing that performance with bated breath, fearing that she would draw the knife through her ample bosom—a fear that was allayed when Father did the slicing. But she proceeded with such skill and assurance that the knife invariably did its intended work and no more.

When we had been provided with bread and onions, Mother gave each of us a bit of cheese, about the size of a quarter slice of apple, and repeated the ritual. The sign of the cross was by way of thanksgiving for the daily bread.

The bread was coarse, compounded of wheat flour and its various substitutes. It was also usually stale because for lack of fuel it was baked twice a month; but it was nourishing and sufficient. The cheese was of good quality. The onions taken from the garden were fresh, sweet and plentiful. These and the cheese were the *companatico* for the meal. The word, from the Latin *cum panis,* refers, in Italy, to whatever complements bread at dinner, for bread there is, literally, the staff of life. Quantitatively, it is the bulk of every meal, much more than what is eaten with it. Thus, when the *companatico* was something as precious and expensive as cheese, such as meat, it was served with the same dreaded injunction.

It was a land of scant natural resources, where the bare necessities of life for the masses were hard to come by; where there were no handouts, no food stamps, no food banks, no communal provision for the destitute. In such circumstances I lived my early childhood, and learned from infancy that self-reliance is the stern but salutary condition to survival. We, more fortunate than many others, were never without bread. What we lacked were the various companaticos—if I may enlarge the meaning of that word—that invest life with a certain minimum grace and dignity: adequate living quarters and decent clothes for the body, an occasional sweet, an occasional loaf of the sort of bread the privileged ate regularly. These, and the possibility of improving our lot by the sweat of our brow, were what we lacked. Thus, we lived in an age and place when it was necessary to *fare a miccino.* Are we, in America, at the threshold of such an age, when we may be driven by necessity to lessen the burden of the lean years ahead by depending less on the supermarket and exercising a greater degree of ingenuity and self-reliance in providing for the dinner table? More on this later.

By a series of lucky breaks, I have lived the last seven decades in an environment where life's companaticos have been far and away more than necessary to live an essentially good life, completely purged of the fear of want. The first bit of luck was to have been born of parents whose solicitude for the welfare of their children was exemplary. In their search for better bread and more companatico, they left a land of penury and settled in a land of abundance: the incredibly opulent Pacific Northwest in the U.S.A. That was the second lucky break. The rest, too numerous to enumerate, are reflected in my current well-being as an Emeritus Professor of English at the University of Washington, now engaged in this labor of love and contentment.

The date of our arrival in this terrestrial paradise is recorded in the family archives as November 11, 1913. I was ten years of age. In the winter of 1914, I began my study of the English language in the public school of McCleary, in the state of Washington. Guided by sensitive, kind teachers of archetypical competence—another lucky break—I was prepared to begin my teaching career at the University in the summer of 1927. In 1948 I published my first book, *The Unprejudiced Palate*. The second chapter was titled "The Discovery of Abundance." Since my discovery occurred in 1914, the word "abundance" was a fair description of a land which Charles Beard, writing at about that time, said was blessed with the greatest natural endowment of any nation in the world.

The fertile plains, the virgin forests, the vast and apparently inexhaustible deposits of coal, minerals, petroleum; the fish-rich coastal and inland waters; the variety of favorable climate: these were the material constituents of the natural endowment, the bread-and-butter realities of the discovery by a young immigrant lad. Years ahead, when I learned that a man does not live by bread alone, I enlarged the meaning of abundance to include certain tangible, spiritual realities that assured one of a proprietary interest in the natural endowment: the opportunity and the right to take from it, by the sweat of one's brow, whatever measure was appropriate to well-being and self-realization.

And here I have in mind the inexpressibly precious heritage bequeathed by the Founding Fathers to posterity. Building with unerring vision on the Magna Carta, their ancestral heritage, they proclaimed to all mankind the immutable principles of political economy written into the Declaration of Independence, the Constitution, and its first ten amendments. Collectively, these documents constitute the firm foundation of our nation, and what we are pleased to call the American Way of Life.

Such was the total abundance I had discovered when I published my first book, and in which I had been granted a proprietary interest when, during my twenty-first year, my petition for citizenship was honored. The magnitude of that natural endowment may be fairly described as fullness to overflowing.

The haven to which Father had brought his family was a pioneer milltown in the Grays Harbor region of the state of Washington. It was a typical company town, engaged in a combined logging and milling operation. Logs from the virgin forest were processed in a sawmill situated about three hundred yards from our house. The superintendent of the logging camp sent only the perfect logs to the mill. Giant conifers, as much as fifteen feet in diameter, were cut down several feet above ground level. Trees that, for whatever reason, were deemed imperfect, were left where they had been felled. The best were trimmed and cut into transportable lengths up to about twenty feet or so of the tip end. Thus, of every tree that was sent to the mill, a considerable fraction was left, along with trees rejected and others ruined by the logging operation, as a tangle of ruin on the forest floor. That overflow was one measure of the abundance.

In squaring the logs for cutting into lumber, the head sawyer in the mill followed the same policy as the logging superintendent. Some of the rejected timber was used as fuel for the mill's power plant; the rest was sent by a conveyor belt to an ever-lasting bonfire. The huge conveyor was a V-shaped trough, eighteen inches wide at the base, four feet at the top, and some two hundred feet in length. It was cradled on a framework of steel which started at ground level and rose to an altitude of about eighty feet at the terminal end, above the burning heap below. In the trough revolved an endless chain of massive links to which one-foot lengths of four-by-four were bolted at intervals of ten feet.

Into that conveyor, for ten hours a day, six days a week, for years and years, was dumped all the lumber deemed unfit for the market. The bulk of the refuse consisted of the outer slabs of logs with bark several inches thick. The rest was rejected samples of all the dimensions that were cut: girders, beams, two-by-twelves, four-by-fours, whatever the market required. The overflow of abundance was returned to the land as ashes. Since these operational practices were repeated in the hundreds of logging camps and mills, and since thousands of square miles of conifer forest in the west were still intact, consider the magnitude of that abundance and the magnitude of the overflow left as waste for posterity.

And there were other spectacular manifestations of abundance—fullness to overflowing—in the America of the relatively recent past. When we settled on what was for us an earthly paradise, land was as abundant as lumber. Under the provisions of the Homestead Act, citizens and intended citizens who were of age and householders were offered 160 acres of the public domain. In certain western states, Washington among them, that grant was later increased to 360 acres. Under the provisions of the Timber and Stone Act, one could buy 160 acres of timber and stone land for two dollars and a half an acre. Three decades before we arrived in the Pacific Northwest, 155 million acres of public land had been granted to the railroads, much of which in the western states was timber and stone land. And the railroads, in turn, sold it to various entrepreneurs. In the first decade of this century, one railroad sold 900,000 acres to a timber company for six dollars an acre.

When the timber on the land thus acquired had been cut, the land became stump land, available for one or two dollars an acre. Had my father been as shrewd as a German immigrant neighbor who bought such land and left his children a fortune, I might now be a fat cat instead of a retired school teacher. His reasoning for abstaining from such speculation was beyond reproach: the overflow of land was as abundant as the overflow of wood, and we had more of both than we needed. The quarter acre on which our house was built was adjacent to a large meadow of rich bottom land that had never been cultivated. We could have bought it for a pittance. But there was no need to buy it, since it was there for anyone to use gratis. Furthermore, on the stump land of the surrounding hills and in the streams that drained them, was a rich harvest of game and fish easily caught and brought to the dinner table. At certain times of the year, salmon could be taken from the shallow streams with the bare hands; and the hunt for rabbits and game birds was never a failure. In the midst of such plenty, what was the relevance of a title to land, since we could have its use and its yield? Thus Father reasoned, wisely, as I now believe.

And there was fullness to overflowing of another sort. The present supermarket, with its coded pricing system, precut meat wrapped in cellophane, and checkout stations, is a sophistication then unimagined. The grocery clerk took one's order and filled it from the shelves. When it was substantial, he invariably added something as a bounty. And the butcher shop also proclaimed the land's richness. Meat was generously cut to one's specifications from the quartered animal in the showcase; and at the butcher's back, one might see the unskinned carcass of a steer, a calf, or a lamb suspended from the ceiling on huge iron hooks. He did the skinning during the intervals between waiting on customers. And he, too, added something to a substantial order: an entire beef shank or a pig's trotters. The

variety meats, what the English call offal—heart, kidney, liver, lungs, tripe—were freely given to anyone who was barbarian enough to eat them. Needless to say, the Pellegrinis lived, in part, on the overflow, and lived very well.

I have recorded the phenomena of the landscape of my early years in America for the reason that, collectively, they seemed to me an extended symbol of the nation's overall abundance: a cornucopia of the principal resource systems of the world—land, water, food, fuel, minerals; the whole of what Charles Beard called the natural endowment. The fabled wealth of the nation, coupled with its tangible spiritual realities, had been affirmed and celebrated with abiding faith and love of the land by Walt Whitman:

> Fecund America . . . !
> Thou envy of the globe! thou miracle!
> Thou, bathed, choked, swimming in plenty,
> Thou lucky Mistress of the tranquil barns . . .
> Thou mental, moral orb . . . !
> As a strong bird on pinions free,
> Joyous, the amplest spaces heavenward cleaving,
> Such be the thought I'd think of thee, America . . . .

The nation's fecundity, celebrated by the poet more than half a century before I discovered it, was in no way visibly diminished in 1914. In some ways it had increased, since the forests were fifty years older and still virtually intact. However, a decade or so later, at the height of what historians have appropriately called the "roaring twenties," the assault on the natural endowment was beginning to proceed at such a pace that social scientists gifted with foresight warned that, unless prudence prevailed over exploitative ambition, the endowment would be seriously diminished. The data that occasioned the warning were impressive. Americans, swimming in plenty in the vastness of the New Land, where everything was big, had made a cult of mere bigness, of quantity, of acquisition, of keeping abreast of the Joneses. They created buildings that scraped the skies, dwellings bigger than complete comfort required, big motorcars of such power and speed that their full use had to be forbidden by law. They devised techniques and diets for breeding and feeding animals for the table to increase their bulk, largely in terms of fat that would be left on the dinner plate. They used the resources of applied science to increase the size of produce, and gave the result the name of P. T. Barnum's elephant: Jumbo. And the idiom of the marketplace, the world of affairs, reflected the national obsession with bigness: Let's put it over *big*, make a *big* splash, the *big* shot. And since the jumbo potato was more than one could eat, the pursuit of bigness entailed such waste that the garbage of New York City was enough to feed the city of Naples. Stuart Chase said it all nearly fifty years ago in *The Tragedy of Waste*.

The quantity, of course, was there; and since the hustler could so easily make it in a big way, success came to be equated with acquisition, the accumulation of worldly goods. Hence, the exaltation of what William James called the "bitch goddess success." And success thus conceived, often so easily attained, shared by many in various degrees, generated a national euphoria, a pervasive Panglossian optimism, an unshakable certainty that in this best of all possible worlds, America was the best of all possible countries—the best for its unequaled standard of living, reckoned in terms of luxuries and creature comforts. (Little was said about America's spiritual realities; but they were there, intact, and underpinning the materialities.)

One dinner to which I was invited, and which I have never forgotten, reflected perfectly the belief that the current abundance was inexhaustible. We were in the sixth year of prohibition. The host of the dinner was an Italian bootlegger. His guests of honor were city and county officials whose duty was the enforcement of the Volstead Act. The whiskey was Old Grandad and Old Taylor. The menu was Italian: antipasti, clear broth, ravioli, fried chicken, roast pork, fried zucchini and artichokes, escarole salad, plenty of bread, gallons of wine, baskets of fruit, various kinds of cheese, coffee and brandy. And when bellies were full and belt buckles loosened, the host distributed fifty-cent cigars and fired them with a flaming dollar bill.

Groaning with satiety, the guests leaned back in their chairs, drew lustily on their expensive cigars, and flicked the ashes on the food left on the dinner plates. The host, who had been a penniless peasant in the old country, smiled complacently and said, "America ees gude." Then to me, in Italian, and with a nod toward his guests, *"In America, il dollaro compra tutto."* In America the dollar buys everything. That was all he had learned about the heritage of the Founding Fathers!

What an appropriate symbol, that culinary extravaganza, for the roaring twenties, at a time when the nation was "bathed, choked, swimming in plenty." The feeling that there was no ebbing of the flood tide of plenty, no end to the nation's prosperity, no limits to the achievements of science and technology, reached a certain peak of intensity in the decade following World War I. Historians have defined the totality of that period as "business civilization." And President Coolidge, in office six years of that decade, gave that description the highest political sanction by his historic declaration that the "business of America is business." Had the president been endowed with as much wisdom as silence, he might have warned the nation that the business entailed a dangerous drain on the country's natural resources, and needless waste.

And by a regrettable coincidence, after the end of World War II, two decades later, once again the business of America was business—in a really big way and with a more alarming drain on the natural endowment. In 1947, the value of goods and services produced in the nation reached the unprecedented figure of $225 billion. And we had the atom bomb. With the rest of the world in disarray, no one questioned America's supremacy as a world power in 1947 and for a few years thereafter. The Panglossian Euphoria, a little subdued by the vicissitudes of the intervening decades, once again defined the mood and temper of the nation during the next two decades: A great democracy, bathed, choked, swimming in plenty. And then a sudden change. The energy crisis! And for the first time in the nation's history, the word on everyone's lips was scarcity.

Why sudden? Simply because we had failed to heed the warning of the prophets who had seen it coming. The diminution of the natural endowment had begun with its waste: giant conifers cut six feet above ground level; "imperfect" trees left on the forest floor to rot; the conveyor belt disgorging "imperfect" lumber on the ever-lasting bonfire; the public domain given to reckless exploiters; the fertile plains left to the mercy of the weather, drained of their nutrients, and impoverished; all resources fed into the jaws of bigness and conspicuous consumption. What, at long last, made the change from abundance to scarcity visible worldwide, but especially in the United States, was a postwar raid of unprecedented magnitude on what remained of the basic resource systems of the Earth. Richard Barnet, in *The Lean Years*, said: "In the thirty-five years following the surrender of Germany and Japan, the industrial world has used more petroleum and non-fuel minerals than had been consumed in all previous human history. The United States has bent, burned, or melted about forty percent of the world's non-renewable materials in those years." Hence, the hitherto unknown phenomenon in America known as scarcity.

Its reality is beyond dispute. During the past decade, scholars, working individually or as teams in research foundations, have been at work trying to determine the current status of natural resources. The historian Henry Steele Commager recently reported some of their findings as follows:

> Every year territory the size of the state of Maine is lost to desert; within the next quarter century the world's forests will decline by one third; its water—necessary for farming and sustaining life in the streams and the ocean—by one fourth, and its oil reserves will be depleted by one half. At the current rates of destruction, between a half million and two million species now on earth will be extinguished. We can look forward to a progressive degradation and impoverishment of the earth's total resources.

These predictions and the current reality of scarcity pose grave problems, national and international. They also pose a problem of lesser gravity to each one of us as individual Americans, who have taken more or less for granted the highest standard of living of any nation in the world. What can we do as individuals, what must we do, to lessen the burden of scarcity?

Given the limitations of my own competence and credentials, I am concerned only with the problem you and I must confront; and here I hope to propose some creative suggestions. Scarcity is not a temporary distemper of the economy as was the Great Depression. For good or ill, it is the shape of the future; and we must learn to live with it, without sacrificing what is necessary to live happily, in comfort and dignity. Petroleum and minerals are finite and no longer abundant; it will be centuries before trees planted today attain the size of the forest giants that have been cut. Water and arable land are getting scarce. These data are so beyond dispute that social scientists are at work designing the contours of what they call a "post-petroleum civilization." Note, for example, *The Lean Years: Politics in the Age of Scarcity,* by Richard Barnet; *Small is Beautiful,* by E. F. Schumacher; and *Ecology and the Politics of Scarcity,* by William Ophuls. Furthermore, the nation's home builders, meeting in convention recently, gave tacit approval to "small is beautiful" when they decided that the dream house of the future will be limited to a thousand square feet. And that means no more frills and extras, such as dens, recreation rooms, and two or more bathrooms.

Thus, the question I raised at the beginning of this inquiry—Are we in America at the threshold of the age of *fare a miccino?*—may be answered in the affirmative. Henceforth it will be necessary to take life's companaticos in tinier bites than we have been accustomed to in the past. And this can be done with a certain gaiety, by adding to, rather than subtracting from, the creative and wholesome pleasures of life. For, notwithstanding scarcity, and compared with the many regions in the world that are haunted by the specter of hunger, America is still a land of relative plenty. The lean years require of us who are so fortunately placed in this blessed land no more than that we purge our lives of the frills and extras we once thought necessary, and that we welcome the opportunity to explore the virtue of self-reliance and engross the pleasures inherent in it.

Some of the purging is done for us by the nation's economy. Automobiles and houses are made smaller than was once thought necessary. We now get from here to there not in the quickest possible way, but at a speed that is regulated by law. An economy that reflects the shrinking of the natural endowment tends to regulate the consumption of energy in our dwellings; heat in office and school buildings is turned off or held to a minimum on weekends and holidays. Water departments in urban centers are exploring possible conservation measures, such as decreasing the outflow of water in bathrooms.

Such imposed restrictions are sensible, and no one suffers by them. However, when conservation is voluntarily assumed, not as a temporary expedient, but as a way of life, freshly motivated by a new sense of stewardship, by the realization that we hold in trust for posterity the total patrimony of Nature whence we derive what we need toward well-being, then we shall understand and enthusiastically approve what Montaigne meant when he said that our "Great and glorious masterpiece is to live appropriately."

And what does this mean? I suggest that the very essence of living appropriately, in an age of scarcity, is living in harmony with Nature. Use its bounty with prudence. Renew what is renewable. The soil is a community of organisms. Respect them. When you take down a tree, plant another in its place. Respect the integrity of lakes and rivers. By virtue of their metabolic processes, plants respire oxygen in our atmosphere. Add to the process by planting where you have space. Return all organic waste matter to the soil. In these creative ways, none of which imposes what could be called a burden, we shall contribute significantly toward maintaining what ecologists call the balance of Nature. And that in itself, an integral part of living appropriately, can be an inexhaustible source of pleasure.

All that I have noted thus far constitutes a firm, empirical basis for a necessary and desirable reorientation of our way of life, in accommodating to the lean years ahead with more rather than with less pleasure and well-being. The economist Kenneth Boulding, as long as two decades ago, warned that "Far from scarcity disappearing, it will be the dominant aspect of society; every grain of sand will have to be treasured, and the waste and profligacy of our own day will seem so horrible that our descendents will hardly be able to think of us."

Must we then despair? Not at all, since the alternative is heavy with the promise of a richer life. Instead of *getting* something as the traditional measure of one's personal success, we shall have the unexplored opportunity of *becoming* something: better citizens, better members of the human community. Given the means to live in decency and comfort, free of the fear of want, happiness is never the necessary consequence of living in a mansion, while it is always the necessary consequence of being esteemed as a good human being by one's fellows. And one is more likely to raise an exemplary family in a five-room house than in one of thirty maintained by servants.

These observations are neither original nor profound; but they derive from the collective and unerring wisdom of mankind; and if scarcity roots them deeply in our consciousness, then all hail the lean years! The unfailing source of life's enrichment must be sought within the self. Whether there is a transcendent purpose in life, ordained in a Heaven above the heavens, is uncertain. What is certain is that we are here for a little day and then cease being what we have been. And while we are here, given adequate food, clothing, and shelter, we must explore the virtue of self-reliance and seek happiness, felicity, tranquility in symbiotic relationships with our fellows rather than in mere acquisition of material things. In living thus we shall be in harmony with Nature, for symbiosis is one of its biological principles. Let us keep this fact of Nature constantly at the center of our consciousness, for as it relates to the art of living, it is the Truth of truths.

George Eliot proclaimed this revelation, for it is no less, in *Silas Marner*. The old miserly weaver had sought happiness in hoarding gold; but what he had sought in vain he found in nurturing an infant whom a kind providence had left at his door. And Robert Herrick to the same effect in

"Meat Without Mirth":

> Eaten I have; and though I had good cheer,
> I did not sup, because no friends were there.
> Where mirth and friends are absent when we dine
> Or sup, there wants the incense and the wine.

And finally, Jean Paul Sartre, having tortured his mind with a relentless search for the meaning of existence, having explored existentialism and Marxism, finally embraced such traditional values as fraternity and the family. In his last months, he said: "Today, I consider that everything which occurs in one's consciousness in a given moment is necessarily tied to, often engendered by, the existence of others. What is real is the relationship between thee and me." Precisely! In any given place the human family is an ecosystem composed of interdependent members. And the art of living together is the art that governs that interdependence.

These observations, drawn from the collective wisdom of mankind, constitute the aesthetic and ethical sanction for what I propose as creative, individual ways of responding to the lean years by adding to daily living some hitherto insufficiently explored sources of pleasure: congenial and fruitful labor in the garden, the kitchen, and the cellar. Some have been compelled to resort to such labor by scarcity, an increasing and salutary aversion to junk food, and by the mounting cost of living. Note, for example, the growth of the pea-patch movement, the phenomenon known as organic gardening, the current emphasis on do-it-yourself. Such efforts are all to the good; they accomplish certain desirable ends.

But such labor is also its own reward; it satisfies an inward need felt, I am sure, in varying degrees of urgency by all of us: the urge to live day by day in the lively awareness that we are doing what is right, that we are being creative, productive, as self-reliant as circumstances permit. And the labor I suggest in the garden, the kitchen, and the cellar, is of the sort that satisfies this need. It adds something to Nature's cornucopia; and it is pleasant, gay, often exciting in the results achieved. For what labor yields more sensory, daily pleasure than that which brings to the table one's own produce, a dinner that inspires praise, and a bottle of wine that quickens the pulse, clears the arteries, and makes the heart glad?

There is yet another virtue, in the labor here suggested, that in these troubled days of various alienations, when the traditional stability of the family is threatened, requires special attention. Remember Sartre: "What is real is the relationship between thee and me." The ethic that governs that relationship, that makes it genuinely symbiotic, reciprocally enriching, must be learned in the home. The labor in the garden, the kitchen, and the cellar is familial labor. Wherever there are children, their participation in it, their enthusiasm for it, must be encouraged. They will respond, if taught by example rather than exhortation. Learning by doing, in an ambiance that is collectively creative and warm, as imperceptibly as they grow to maturity, they will learn the ethic that governs human relationships, that what is real is the relationship between thee and me.

Welcome, then, to the lean and happy days ahead. And lest you should forget the scarcity that occasioned the discovery of these transcendent values, let me note two final manifestations of it. Six decades ago wood as fuel littered the landscape in this timber-rich Pacific Northwest. A bundle of such fireplace wood, no larger than a child can carry with ease and scarcely enough to warm the bricks in the fireplace, now costs two dollars. And to the list of variety meats such as tripe, now as expensive per pound as prime beef ten years ago, have been added steer's testicles. Are you up to dining on those purplish goodies the size and shape of avocados? My butcher tells me that they are much in demand by knowing gourmets and gentlemen whose virility is in decline. Unfortunately, since a steer has only two, these symbols of scarcity are themselves scarce. However, it is barely possible that geneticists may produce a species of steers equipped with four, six, or even a dozen. Possible? I wouldn't bet on it. We will simply have to make do with what we have. So, on with our creative and happy labors in the garden, the kitchen, and the cellar.

My intent in what follows is to suggest, and it is offered with a certain diffidence. For who am I that I should tell you precisely how you shall live? And if I urge these creative labors with a certain passion, it is because my belief in their ethical propriety and relevance to the lean years is profound. Accept my recommendations only if you find them congenial after you have examined them with utmost care. Remember that what I have in mind is the full use of our individual potential and the attainment of the maximum degree of self-reliance.

In establishing your garden and tending it thereafter, and in doing your kitchen work, avoid, wherever possible, the use of power tools and electrical kitchen utensils. Entailing as they do a drain on energy and being not in the least indispensable in the performance of garden and kitchen work, all such gadgetry is a species of waste and needless expense. Learn how to manage the simple tools of the peasant: the shovel, the rake, the hoe, the hand trowel, and use your own energy.

Nature has provided us the most perfect of all tools, the hands. Let us bear this in mind, explore the manifold uses of this marvelous gift of Nature, and reduce to an absolute minimum the use of all energy-consuming gadgets. And here I am thinking of certain Italian ladies, who refuse to use a pasta machine, because they insist that they can make pasta more quickly and better with their hands. And they can, for I have seen them do it. When I asked a neighborhood baker in his eighties why he did not use an electric mixer, he told me that when he could no longer do it with his hands he would quit baking.

The ladies and the baker, in refusing to use a machine to do what they have always done with their hands, are not merely slaves to habit and skeptical of new methods; they know the immense satisfaction they derive in producing a hand-crafted product which no machine could in any way improve, in earning their bread, so to speak, by the sweat of their brow. If they could rationalize what they know intuitively, they would say that they and the matter which they transform are one; and that when the transformation is completed, the hands and the mind that directed them are embodied in the pasta and the loaf of bread. To know that satisfaction, that rare species of pleasure, one must make an art of the use of one's hands, become an artisan.

There was once in the world of fiction a magic city

where one might have whatever one desired; but if one chose a machine, one was required to live with it for the rest of his life. We, too, have chosen the machine, and the danger we must avoid is such dependence on it that we become a subspecies of button-pushers. Used for heavy, dirty work such as draining a swamp, the machine is a blessing; used to slice bread or a roast, it is a vulgarity, a waste of energy and precious materials. The purveyors of such gadgetry spend millions of dollars to persuade us to buy what we do not need; and our response to their blandishments must be a firm refusal to buy.

The ultimate refinement in technology was achieved a generation ago. In August, 1945, the press announced that a new force of Nature had been harnessed. Having created it, man must live with it. Its experimental use for evil has already been accomplished. To what end will it be used tomorrow? The choice is ours.

The violet and the daffodil are in bloom. Nature's sap is beginning to flow. The birds are chirping and twittering their epithalamia. In silent protest against the needless use of all gadgetry, and the evil use of that new force in Nature, I shall take my spade, turn the sod, and press the replicating seed into the soil. Do ye likewise.

TWO

The Garden

TO ESTABLISH and maintain a productive kitchen garden requires no special talent. The labor is restorative and the procedures are easily within one's competence. In other words, there is no one who lacks the wit necessary to become an accomplished gardener. And yet there is the discouraging myth of the green thumb. Nonsense! A green thumb is a convenient metaphor that describes one who has learned what to do and does his work well. There are, to be sure, a few simple horticultural procedures that one must learn, if he does not know them already. I refer the novitiate to my book, *The Food-Lover's Garden* (Knopf, New York, and Madrona Publishers, Seattle) for a detailed treatment of the subject. There are also monographs on the vegetable garden available from the U.S. Department of Agriculture and its counterpart in the several states. My intent here is only to spur you on to the effort by giving an account of the dollar value of a properly managed kitchen garden; and I can do this with some precision by presenting an inventory of my own garden. As for the rest, where there is a will there is a way.

But first a word about gardening as an avocation and its cultural propriety. Ralph Waldo Emerson, that probing and far-ranging American writer, sought and found in garden labor the appropriate means to calm his mind.

> I know no means of calming the fret and perturbation into which too much sitting, too much talking, brings me, so perfect as labor. I have no animal spirits; therefore, when surprised by company and kept in a chair for many hours, my heart sinks, my brow is clouded and I think I will run for Acton woods, and live with the squirrels henceforward. But my garden is nearer, and my good hoe, as it bites the ground, revenges my wrongs, and I have less lust to bite my enemies. I confess I work at first with a little venom, lay to a little unnecessary strength. But by smoothing the rough hillocks, I smooth my temper; by extracting the long roots of the piper-grass, I draw out my own splinters; and in a short time I can hear the bobolink's song and see the blessed deluge of light and color that rolls around me.

Andrew Borde, physician to "his prepotent Majeste" King Henry VIII, an English gentleman who minded his belly very studiously and very carefully, went on record with this practical observation: "It is a commodious and pleasant thing to a mansion to have an orchard of sundry fruits; but it is more commodious to have a fair garden, replete with herbs of aromatic and redolent savour."

We have pork cutlets in the cooler. The dinner hour is nigh and my wife and I are hungry. Hunger in a gardener has a way of relating to the garden. How shall we enhance the flavor of the cutlets? What vegetable shall we have with them? We go to the fair garden, take from it garlic and leaves of sage. We mince these, add a bit of olive oil, lave the cutlets with the savory mixture and cook them slowly in the skillet. The vegetable we have chosen is spinach. Having blanched and drained and finely minced it, we remove the cooked cutlets from the skillet and finish cooking the spinach in the savory meat juices. This done, salt and pepper to taste, we arrange the cutlets over the spinach and let the two marry over low heat while we pull the cork from a bottle of red wine. Then we sit to supper, count our blessings, and wonder what fat cat is dining as well.

Such a dinner, so simple and yet so elegant, is routine in our home; and it can be so in yours. Note what a fair garden contributes to it. Do you find it attractive? Does it make your mouth water? Of course! Then roll up your sleeves, take tools in hand and establish a commodious and fair garden replete with redolent savor. The size, location, and soil are first considerations. How extensive shall the garden be? That depends on how much space is available and how much one can comfortably manage. It must not be so large that its keeping will become a burden. My own is a plot thirty by fifty: fifteen hundred square feet. As an easily manageable kitchen garden, it is more than adequate in productivity. A more extensive area I could not till properly in the time I have after my daily professional work is done.

Its location is not a matter of choice, for the growth of herbs and vegetables requires full sun. Six hours of sun daily are indispensable. Less than that spells frustration. So plan accordingly. Furthermore, there must not be large trees in the peripheral area, for their roots are far-ranging and will take from the soil much of its nutrients.

The composition of the soil must be adequate—a foot or more deep, fertile, friable, loose, easily crumbled. Its type is not so important as that it be well drained, adequately supplied with humus, organic matter retentive of moisture, and free of stones. So-called heavy soil, clay or hardpan, or all sand, will not do. And once the garden area has been established, it must be constantly replenished with humus, organic material which consists of partially or wholly decayed vegetable matter that provides nutrients for plants and aids the soil in retaining moisture. This can be done by repeatedly spading into the soil the garden's considerable waste of vegetable matter, including weeds. We keep a bucket under the kitchen sink into which we put all fruit and vegetable trimmings; and when the bucket is full, its contents are immediately spaded into the soil. Such land husbandry, faithfully practiced year after year, results in rich, dark, loose soil in which the fussiest of vegetables happily flourish.

Well-rotted animal waste, collectively known as barnyard manure, is the natural and ecologically appropriate plant food. Dropped freely in nature, it is incorporated into the soil, whence it is taken by the flora and thus becomes an integral part of the ecosystem. The same result is achieved by the virtually self-sustaining farmer who, when he cleans the shelters of his various animals, masses the waste near the barn, where it ferments and rots. Thus properly aged, it is incorporated by plowing into the land early in the spring. This method of soil fertilization and enrichment is the natural way, the organic way. Thus treated, the soil is constantly improved and never exhausted.

For this reason, the gardener is urged to use barnyard manure. He may find it at certain nurseries or at some conveniently located dairies. Where it is not available, composted steer and chicken manure, sold in forty- or fifty-pound bags, is an adequate substitute. Whether the one or the other, it should be spread over the garden area early in the spring and incorporated into the soil by spading. When properly spaded so that sod and manure are overlaid with subsoil, the area must be thoroughly raked, the function of which is to crumble the hillocks, remove the stones and other debris, and effect an even, level surface preparatory to planting and sowing. For the time and manner of sowing the various seeds, note the directions given on the seed packet. Generally, the soil is prepared early in the spring when it is dry enough to be worked; and the seeds for early crops, such as peas, spinach, lettuce, and root vegetables, are sown when the danger of a deep freeze is past.

The art of the accomplished gardener, his craft, his handiwork, consists in doing all those things properly and with ease. Its mastery requires time. Don't be discouraged if first results are less than perfect. Remember that there is world enough and time; that the labor is creative, pleasant, and refreshing; that the end result is enrichment of the dinner hour, money saved, and the profound satisfaction of doing something toward living in harmony with Nature.

If I had the pleasure—and it would be nothing less than pure pleasure—of showing you my garden, which I have been tending for exactly forty years, I would first call your attention to the soil, loose, easily crumbled in the hand, dark with the manure and organic material incorporated in it, alive with worms and the necessary microorganisms, a soil that conforms in every particular to the description of the ideal garden soil given above. You would need no more than the most elementary knowledge of soils to perceive immediately its fertility. And I would ask you to note the overall cleanliness of the area, for both aesthetic and hygienic reasons. Rubble such as decaying vegetation, which is the necessary waste of plant growth toward maturity, is offensive to the eye and a breeding refuge for pests. Therefore, weeds are removed and buried as soon as they appear, and especially before they bear the replicating seeds. The dead lower leaves of green vegetables are also removed and buried; and when vegetables are harvested, their trimmings are similarly disposed of.

The performance of these little tasks is not merely being fussy and unnecessarily meticulous. It enhances productivity, facilitates pest control, and adds to the loveliness of the "fair garden replete with herbs of aromatic and redolent savour." Furthermore, the labor itself is pleasant; as pleasant, I dare say, as the labor of a loving mother in tending the infant child. And if it is not immediately so, if one finds it boring and arduous, an act of will to find it congenial may help. At any rate, it is worth a try. For interest in doing something normally follows having learned to do it well. I insist on this from a stubborn refusal to believe that there could possibly be anyone so radically different from me that he could not learn to enjoy gardening.

Even such a one may be persuaded to endure what he does not enjoy because the effort will pay ample dividends. One may infer the extent of the possible gain from an account of the dollar value of the produce of my own kitchen garden. And to that I now turn my attention. It is now mid-June 1982. The price of the various vegetables hereafter quoted was checked at the supermarket this day;

and the morning paper assures us that food prices are rising. I must also note that I live in the Pacific Northwest, where there is ample water and the climate is right for green and most root vegetables, but not for hot-weather produce such as tomatoes, peppers, okra, and eggplant. It is also noteworthy that winters here are normally so mild that certain hardy vegetables, rooted in late summer, may be harvested in late fall, early winter, and even the following spring. However, this advantage is countered in warmer climates, where crops come to maturity more rapidly and thus make possible successive sowings. So, on balance, the dollar value of a kitchen garden of a given size is substantially the same regardless of its location.

Let us now appraise my garden as a creative assault on scarcity. I cannot give its exact worth in dollars; but I may give enough to warrant a fairly accurate conclusion. The culinary art, which I shall discuss in the following chapter, requires the use of considerable quantities of shallots and garlic. No doubt one can live well enough without the use of these very expensive flavoring agents. However, they are the basic ingredients in the cuisine promoted by such accomplished teachers of cookery as Julia Child and James Beard; and I assume that readers of these pages who are intent on improving their cuisine will need quantities of them no less extensive than the amount I use. Given the ever-growing interest in so-called gourmet cooking, the assumption is fairly safe. And here is how I produce our yearly supply of these and its value in dollars at current prices.

Toward the end of February or early March, depending on the weather, I planted 130 shallot bulbs and 100 cloves of garlic. These had been saved from last year's harvest. As result of what is known as selective breeding in plant and animal husbandry, the policy of always using the most perfect stock for reproduction, the bulbs and cloves I planted were large and sound. Since these multiply in growing, each bulb will produce a cluster of about six or more; and each clove an aggregate of about ten or more. Thus, at maturity, about mid-July, I will harvest, in round numbers, 900 shallots and 1,000 cloves of garlic, about three of each for every day of the year. An abundant and luxuriant harvest, more than enough, including a reserve of reproductive stock for next year.

From past experience I know that the yields in pounds will be about forty-five for the one and thirty-five for the other. The current price for shallots and garlic, sold in packets of two or three ounces rather than in bulk, is five dollars a pound for the one and four and a half for the other. Thus the total value of the two crops, again in round numbers, is three hundred eighty dollars. The garden area is fifteen hundred square feet. Bulbs and cloves, set four inches apart in rows six inches apart, are grown on sixty square feet of that area. Do you begin to see the dollar value of such a kitchen garden?

And note what further is grown on those sixty square feet, one twenty-fifth of the total garden area. Three weeks ago I sowed cardoon seeds between the two rows of shallot bulbs. The seeds, approximately the same as sunflower seeds, were spaced fifteen inches apart. These have now germinated, two tiny leaves about a third of an inch long. In about four weeks, when the shallots will be harvested, the cardoon seedlings will be four or five inches long; and thereafter each plant will have ample space to grow to maturity. And when the garlic is harvested at about the same time, turnips and rutabagas, which germinate in about a week, will be sown in the vacated space, a fifteen-foot row of each. With cardoons selling for a dollar and a half a stalk where they are available, and turnips and ruta-bagas priced at fifty cents a pound, the value of the total harvest will be approximately thirty dollars. Since our real-estate tax is eight hundred and fifty dollars, the value of the produce on sixty square feet of this garden area is enough to pay nearly half of it.

And here one may well ask, "What on earth is a car-doon?" The question is appropriate; this vegetable, so highly prized by Mediterraneans and so easily grown, ought to be more widely known. The name derives from the Latin word *carduus,* thistle. And that is precisely what the cardoon is, a domesticated thistle. Morphologically, it resembles celery, but giant celery such as Gulliver may have seen in the land of the Brobdingnagians; in taste, it re-minds one of the artichokes. It achieves maturity in five or six months. Its stalks or ribs will then be huge and fernlike in structure, the outer ones three or four feet in length. The lower portion, one or two inches wide, is bare and fleshy like the ribs of a celery. The upper flares out with leafy ser-rated notches on both sides of the central spine. At that stage of growth, the ribs are bound together in a bundle, wrapped with burlap or black plastic two thirds of the way from the ground level, soil is banked around the plant sev-eral inches up from the base, and it is left to attain its edible maturity. In three or four weeks, going into November, the inner ribs, as in celery, will be bleached and succulent

and ready to eat. The heart and core may be eaten raw, dipped in a condiment of lemon juice, oil, a dash of Tabasco sauce, salt and pepper. The sound outer ribs may be cut into three-inch lengths, blanched in salted boiling water, then finished cooking in a light sauce compounded of a bit of minced salt pork, onion, garlic, parsley, and a cup of stock slightly acidulated with lemon juice. Or, for a rare taste treat, the blanched pieces may be coated with a light batter and browned nicely on both sides in a skillet with enough olive oil to cover the bottom. Salt and pepper to taste; and a few drops of lemon juice will enhance the flavor.

When cardoons are bundled and wrapped as described above, now, fully grown, they remain stable for several weeks, so the individual plants may be harvested as needed. When the plant is cut at ground level, the root, deep and woody, remains alive but dormant. The following spring, a new plant rises from the root crown, smaller than the first growth, its ribs more slender. When two or three feet long, these may be cut and cooked as described above. But if they are harvested much later than that, they will be tough and bitter and not edible. Left to complete its life cycle, the plant develops a center stem which attains a height of five or six feet, with a purple-centered flower bud like that of a thistle but much larger and of striking beauty. That is the seed pod, crammed with hundreds of seeds. The plant I saved for my seed supply is now, at mid-June, four feet tall, and the flower bud is just forming. The seeds will attain maturity in late summer. Since a packet of three or four dozen cardoon seeds sells for sixty cents, there is money in that seed pod; or, better still, ample seeds for my many friends who have discovered the cardoon at our dinner table. And this completes the account of what is produced on that small fraction of the garden.

In another fraction, a plot five feet by twenty, I grow twenty artichoke plants. This choice vegetable, always expensive, was developed from the cardoon, which it resembles so closely that only one who knows them well can distinguish one from the other. They are planted two feet apart in two rows three feet apart. Each plant produces four to six artichokes. The price varies from fifty cents to a dollar, according to the season. The average being about seventy-five cents, the total value of my crop is seventy-five dollars. Thus, the dollar value of the two fractions of the garden area is nearly five hundred dollars.

The artichoke plant is a two-crop perennial, one in the spring, the other in the fall. It attains a height of about three feet and a circular leaf spread about three feet in diameter. When well established, normally in the second year after propagation, the root crown sends up as many as a dozen plants of various sizes. The largest each develop a basal rosette cluster of leaves formed like those of the cardoon, though smaller and less fleshy at the base. A stem with several branches rises gradually from the center of the rosette. While the plant is growing toward maturity, a flower bud is formed at the tip of the main stem and, later, at the tip ends of the several branches. These, in their mature state, before flowers and seeds develop, are the edible portions of the plant. These are the artichokes.

Thus the artichoke, like asparagus, beans, and broccoli, is actually the seed pod of the plant. And it has an interesting structure. The bud, when prime for the table, is a compact mass of bracts or scales closely overlaid one upon another and attached at their bases to a round, fleshy receptacle upon which flower and seeds are borne at maturity. The receptacle is slightly concave. The bracts are roughly pear-shaped. They are small on the underside of the receptacle, where it is attached to the stem, become larger as they grow upward all around it, and decrease in size at their tips. When the artichoke is at its best for eating, the bracts are closed tightly into a compact, ovoid bud about the size of a large lemon. As it develops toward maturity, the bracts open at the top like the petals of a rosebud, and the artichoke becomes a purple-centered, thistlelike flower with a seed receptacle about three inches in diameter. At that stage its appeal is purely aesthetic, and the gardener gladly yields it to the flower-garden buff who will use it in his flower arrangements. One is therefore well advised to harvest the artichoke when it is essentially immature, or to avoid buying it at the market when its bracts are completely opened at the top. It is then advertised as a jumbo artichoke and will appeal primarily to one who lives by the quantitative fallacy. It must have been some such aging artichoke that prompted the judgment attributed to Lord Chesterfield: "The artichoke is the only vegetable known of which there is more left when one has finished eating it than when he began."

There will be no such heap of waste when the artichoke is taken at its edible best and prepared for cooking thus: Cut a half inch off the tip. Cutting on the bias with a very sharp knife, shear off the upper tough part of the bracts, rotating the compact bud with one hand as the other moves the knife up and down on the bracts. This operation, which requires some practice to perform effectively, peels the artichoke down to its light yellow edible portion. Work slowly and with care so that you remove the green portion only of each bract. Cut the peeled ovoid in half lengthwise. Since the artichoke is immature, there will be no choke at its center, the cottony fluff that constitutes the upper portion of the seed pod. Cut each half in two slices. Drop them in boiling salted water, being careful not to overcook them. They are best done *al dente,* like properly cooked pasta. Prepare a blend of lemon juice, olive oil, salt and pepper, a few drops of Tabasco sauce in an adequate bowl. Drain the slices and toss them in the blend. Or simply sauté the raw slices in olive oil, lemon juice, garlic, parsley, salt and pepper. Or cut the peeled artichoke in six longitudinal slices, dip them in a light batter and proceed as suggested for the cardoon. Prepare it in any one of these ways, then ask Lord Chesterfield for dinner and politely remind his lordship how little he knows about the way to prepare an artichoke for the table.

Propagation of the artichoke is by root section. If propagated by seed, it tends to revert to its thistle ancestry. As I've mentioned, it is a perennial. When the crop is harvested, the fruit-bearing plant is cut at ground level, and another promptly grows from the root crown. My plants have grown in the same area for more than thirty years. Following the practice of commercial growers, I have renewed the plants every five or six years. This is advisable in order to assure a continuous crop of fine-quality fruit. After the spring harvest, the root, large, branched, deep and woody like that of the cardoon, is extracted, divided into substantial sections and replanted. In the fall these will bear their first crop.

Another satisfactory way of starting new plants, either to add to one's stock or to give some to others, is by plant division. As I have stated above, a healthy root crown, well fertilized preferably by barnyard manure, will produce several plants of various sizes. The largest of these, twenty inches or so in length, may be extracted from the main root, a few inches of foliage clipped from the top, and replanted. When this is done, one must work carefully in the extraction so that the extracted plant has root fibers attached to it. However, this method of propagation requires a full year of growth before the new plant bears fruit; and it does not obviate the need for renewing the plant as suggested above.

And there is more to note in behalf of the artichoke. Derived from the cardoon, structurally resembling it, its ribs also are edible and choice. In the spring and in the fall, when the new plants rise from the root crown to a height of about twenty inches, and their ribs or individual stalks are well formed, they may be taken up and prepared for the table as suggested for the young shoots of the cardoon that emerge in the spring following the harvest of the mature plant. They are edible only when they are young and tender, before the fruit-bearing stem begins to develop. From a root crown that produces several plants, one may take, as thinnings, all but three or four of the largest, leaving these to bear fruit. And now a final note: When the artichoke is harvested, one must take with it about three inches of the stem, for that much of it, thinly peeled, is tender and delicious.

I have dealt in some detail with these two vegetables for several reasons. They belong in the upper aristocracy of herbaceous edibles. And yet they, especially the cardoon, are practically unknown in American households and gardens. The taste for them is not an acquired taste. Friends who have had them at our dinner table have immediately enjoyed them immensely. They are relatively immune to plant diseases and so easily grown. Furthermore, as I have indicated, the edible yield of each plant is so abundant that they deserve a central place in the kitchen-garden economy. Therefore, for these reasons, but principally for their excellence as food, one ought to investigate the possibility of growing them in whatever region one lives. They do require deep, loose, fertile soil, cool sun, and plenty of water.

Next in the order of productivity and dollar value, relative to space, are pole beans. I planted two parallel rows about thirty feet in length. The space between them is four feet. The total area is a hundred and twenty square feet. Set about three feet apart, there are ten poles in each row. Each pole, ten feet high, supports three bean vines, for a total of sixty. Each vine, winding in a right–left spiral according to its mysterious nature, will reach to the top of the pole and then, having no further pole to embrace, will squirm and twist, no doubt in agony, and embrace itself and fellow vines until the longitudinal potential, latent in the seed, is exhausted.

There are various kinds of pole beans. I have chosen Blue Lake and Romani, also called Oregon Horticultural, six poles of the one and fourteen of the other. The Blue Lake will be harvested as green beans, very likely the best of all green beans. Most of the Romani, also prized as green beans before the bean develops in the pod, will be harvested as shell beans when the bean in the pod is mature. A conservative estimate of the total production is fifty pounds of green beans and twenty pounds of shell beans. The current price of fine-quality green beans is eighty cents a pound. A pound of shelled shell beans is about a dollar and a quarter. Thus the value of the beans grown on one hundred and twenty square feet of the garden area is sixty-five dollars. Have you been following the arithmetic? Thus far we have used only two hundred and fifty of the fifteen hundred square feet of soil, and the value of its produce is approximately five hundred dollars. Need I proceed further in this tedious, miserly reckoning of dollars and cents? Have I not proved beyond all doubt that a kitchen garden is a *creative* assault on scarcity? Since there is no sensible urging of the obvious, I shall get on with a summary account of the rest of the produce, with such comments as seem appropriate.

The shell beans are ready for the table when the pod, having achieved full maturity, bulged with total pregnancy, and changed color from green to light brown, begins to wither slightly. But only slightly! It will have lost its drum-tight compactness, feel limber and pliant to the touch, but the shell itself will still be green in texture though not in color, and moist, not in the least dry. At that stage, the bean inside is large, mealy, succulent. As the shell loses its moisture and begins to dry, the bean undergoes the same change and loses its tenderness and succulence. Where that process is well under way, it is best to leave the pod on the vine, to be harvested when completely dry. It is also advisable to leave certain of the best pods, the ones that have from six to eight beans, to dry on the vine for use as seed stock. The advantage of the pole over the bush bean, where space is limited, is greater productivity per square foot of soil.

It's a pity that the shell bean is so little known among gardeners and housewives that it is rarely available at the greengrocer, for its virtue as a protein-rich legume is precisely the virtue of green peas. Larger than the dry variety, more pulpy and succulent, it has a more pleasing flavor and cooks more quickly. All it needs as a condiment when cooked *al dente* in salted water is a quick stir in a bit of hot butter or olive oil flavored with garlic and a mince of fresh thyme. Boiled and creamed, it is the best of all beans as a thickening and flavoring agent in that hearty Italian soup known as minestrone. Furthermore, it is the only vegetable known to me that undergoes no change whatever in the freezer. Shelled directly into an appropriate container, without blanching, shell beans may be kept in the freezer for as long as a year without the slightest diminution in their integrity. And while any variety may be harvested as shell beans, the Romani are choice.

And now a further note on shrewd utilization of space. When I put the bean seeds in the ground in two parallel rows four feet apart, the space they need for their luxuriant growth, I sowed turnips and spinach, a fifteen-foot row of each, between them. Since these germinate and mature more quickly than the beans, they were ready for the table by the time the bean vines were two feet up the pole. Turnip greens and spinach, both of which may be satisfactorily preserved by freezing, sell for fifty cents a bunch; figure, if you must, their dollar value and add it to the value of the beans. Then ponder values that cannot be expressed in dollars and cents.

In the space not accounted for thus far I have grown and harvested, in quantities sufficient for our need, two crops of spinach, two of turnips—these for the greens—

one of chard, one of lettuce. There are now, and soon ready for the pot, a second row of peas, a third crop of turnips, a second of lettuce and chard. Beets, both roots and greens, and green onions are now ready and at their best. Along one border of the garden area is a row of raspberries; along another, a trellised row of Cascade berries. The ones are ripe; the others are beginning to turn black. Both will yield whatever jam we need for the year. For later harvest are a year's supply of dry onions, carrots, leeks, and potatoes, vegetables sown early but which require several months to mature. Cauliflower and Brussels sprouts, transplanted two months ago, are slowly maturing. The several tomato plants are doing well; we now hope for the necessary sun to set and ripen the fruit.

There is yet some space available in the total area; there will be more when the pea vines are cut at ground level, leaving the nitrogen-rich roots in the ground. In that space will be planted during the next week—it is now July 6— curly kale, collards, Savoy cabbage, and broccoli, the young seedlings of which are ready for transplanting in about two weeks. All these vegetables are cold-hardy and will not be ready for use until they have been sweetened and tenderized by the light frosts of late fall and early winter. Mature and stable at that stage, they will be available well into the winter and early spring in such mild climates as that of the Pacific Northwest. A light, early fall of snow does them no harm.

All of these leaf vegetables, constant in the fine cuisine of the south, are excellent in vegetable soups and eaten as greens with pork—roasts, chops, and sausage. Rich in vitamins and minerals, they have the additional virtue of continuous supply, for as the lower, mature leaves are taken, new ones grow on the stem above them. The same is true of chard. Of the second crop, now ready for use, I shall cut the top as needed, three inches above the root. New ones will grow rapidly.

Another leaf vegetable of excellent quality that ought to be better known is chicory. There are several varieties; and, unfortunately, only the more complete seed stores have any of them in stock. But seeds are available of some varieties; and persistence may move your local seed merchant to get them for you. Among Mediterraneans of discriminating taste at the table, a salad of young chicory leaves with an oil and vinegar dressing is considered a classic.

I recommend especially witloof, the chicory also called Belgian endive, for its inner, bleached, compact fold of leaves; and which at six or more dollars a pound is ridiculously and inexplicably expensive. For it is easy to grow; and in deep, loose, fertile soil its growth is luxuriant. We had our first salad from the first crop a few days ago. The leaves are tongue-shaped, now about six inches long, perfect for salads. As the plant grows toward maturity, the leaves may be used as a cooked vegetable. Full-grown, the abundant leaves, the outer ones more than a foot long, may be gathered into a cluster and tied loosely. In time, the inner core will be partly bleached, much like what is sold as Belgian endive. Another way of forming that core, exactly as sold by the greengrocer, is so simple that one wonders why it should be so expensive. When the plant is full-grown, late in the fall, its outer leaves will begin to turn yellow, droop, and die. Its single root will be several inches long, about the size of a parsnip. At that stage the plant is uprooted and replanted. Cut the leaves about an inch above ground level. Working carefully to avoid mutilating the root, extract it, clip off an inch or two from its bottom end, and replant it deep enough so that its top will be covered by ten inches or so of soil. Thus rather harshly treated, it will bide its time, dormant, throughout the winter. Early in the spring, a slight upthrust in the soil crust will indicate that the Belgian endive is formed. Horticulturally, this simply means that the witloof chicory, despite amputation and decapitation, is determined to complete its life cycle. For that is precisely what is happening; if left undisturbed, the plant would grow to a considerable height, bear many blue flowers, a profusion of tiny seeds, then wither and die. Such is one of the many marvels of Nature that the gardener learns to admire, wonder at, and respect.

In taking up the plant for its precious and expensive fold of bleached leaves, one must avoid mutilating the root, for it is edible and choice, more so than the endive itself. Peel it as you would a carrot or a parsnip. Cut it in rather thin slices. Drop them in a bit of boiling salted water and turn off the heat, since they cook very quickly. Drain them and stir them in hot butter or olive oil, with a squeeze of lemon juice and a grind of pepper, and eat them with relish. Since the young leaves of the chicory and the tender root are slightly bitterish, the relish of these may be an acquired taste. If so, it may also be wholesomely addictive. My wife has found them so. She had not tasted such vegetables before she joined her life to that of a Mediterranean; and now she literally craves the root. So do our grown children who, when they were quite young, had no more taste for bitterish vegetables than children generally. Their favorite salad now is chicory and its wild ancestor, the spring dandelion.

There is another treasure in the kitchen garden which deserves the closest attention: the family of culinary herbs. Some are so indispensable in excellent cuisine that where one has only a few square feet of space, he would be well advised to use it only for their cultivation; for they are not generally available at the greengrocer. When have you ever seen fresh rosemary, sage, oregano, tarragon, basil, thyme, English pennyroyal, in the produce section of the supermarket? They are not such exotics as grow only in certain remote nooks of the planet. On the contrary, they may be grown easily anywhere in the country and need no other nutrients than are constant in ordinary soil. The reason why they are not grown commercially, nor brought to market by the truck gardener, is that there is no demand for them. And this means that the run-of-the-mill householder has yet to learn their desirability as flavoring agents in cookery. The following incidents are instructive.

A few years ago, my wife and I dined in London in an intimate Italian family restaurant. When the waiter brought us a platter of potatoes—in the British Isles potatoes are always served willy-nilly—we immediately caught the aroma of fresh rosemary; for they had been pan-fried with garlic and sprigs of that, to us, familiar herb. Pleasantly surprised to be served potatoes thus flavored in London, notwithstanding that the restaurant was Italian, I asked the restaurateur whether he himself had a rosemary bush on the premises; and he told me that an Italian truck gardener, twenty miles out of London, kept him supplied with that and other herbs. He was pleased, of course, that we had noted and appreciated that refinement in his cuisine.

Our son, who occasionally manned the galley on a fishing vessel last season, served potatoes quartered and oven-roasted in olive oil, seasoned with garlic and sprigs of rosemary he had taken aboard from our garden. The crew were delighted; they had never had potatoes so good. The skipper was especially pleased; so pleased, indeed, that he wanted our son to join the crew the following season as the permanent chef. Then, noting the rosemary sprigs, now brown and crisp, asked, "But what in hell are these sticks?" His name was Peterson.

Our daughter, Angela, accomplished in the use of culinary herbs, and her daughter, Sarah, then ten years of age, were walking along a country road in Spain a few years ago. Noting many rosemary bushes growing wild, Angela plucked a twig and handed it to Sarah. "What is this?" she asked. Sarah sniffed it and promptly replied, "Lamb chops." She did not recognize the plant; but the young girl already had an educated palate, and her mother's use of rosemary in lamb cookery had not escaped her. What we may hope for in America's rapidly coming gastronomically of age, is less Petersons who mistake rosemary sprigs for sticks, and more children who mistake them for lamb chops. And this will be the sooner realized as more and more kitchen gardeners grow a variety of culinary herbs.

The word "herb" derives from the Latin *herba*, grass. In botany, herb is the name of those plants the stem or stalk of which dies to the root each year. Such plants are called herbaceous. Among the many varieties of herbs, some are herbaceous and some are deciduous. Some are annuals, some biennials, and some are perennials. A considerable number have well-established culinary value; and of these, several are indispensable in the kitchen garden in the sense that they complete its culinary relevance. For they are, of course, exclusively flavoring agents. And such are the ones I have listed: rosemary, sage, oregano, tarragon, basil, thyme, and English pennyroyal, also known as *Mentha pulegium*. Of the use of these and other more widely known flavoring agents, such as parsley, celery, onion, garlic, I shall have much to say in the next chapter. A word now about their cultivation.

As I have already stated, herbs are easy to grow in any soil and need very little care. Rosemary, sage, oregano, thyme, and tarragon are perennials. In mild climates the first four remain green the entire year. Tarragon does not. Where the winters are severe and the temperature drops below twenty above zero, tarragon should be grown in large containers and brought inside during the winter. Basil is a warm-weather annual. Sown late in May, it will complete its life cycle in early fall. Pennyroyal blooms, bears seeds, and reseeds itself, often appearing in scattered spots in the garden in the spring. The value of these herbs is inestimable; and the kitchen garden that contains them may be considered complete; it is easy to see why the physician of "his prepotent Majeste" considered such a garden to be even more commodious and pleasant than an orchard.

It is now early July. The morning paper informs us that food prices are rising, a totally gratuitous bit of information. Notwithstanding the fact that we are in the season of maximum vegetable production, not a single unit of even the most common variety of vegetables, whether sold by the bunch or the pound, is less than half a dollar. A family of four, dining on hamburger or weenies and an adequate portion of peas or green beans or spinach, will pay as much, or possibly more, for the vegetables as for the meat. By growing one's own produce in an adequate kitchen garden such as I have described, the cost of that dinner could be cut in half. The cautious economists, with no axes to grind, aware of the complexity of the economy and the inscrutable logic of corporate big business, hesitate to endorse any easy formula for putting an end to the inflationary spiral. There is a measure of relief in growing whatever one can for his dinner.

In conclusion, I would urge the more persuasive and compelling reason for adding to one's mode of purposive living the keeping of a kitchen garden: its ecological, aesthetic, and ethical propriety. A love for the soil and the loveliness of its growth; a respect for nature by living in harmony with it; a concern for posterity by adding to rather than subtracting from nature's cornucopia; a continuous striving to become a more worthy member of the human family: these are ancestral virtues, as old as civilized man. And their yield is felicity.

THREE

The Kitchen

GROW your own; cook your own; make your own wine. Such is the threefold imperative. Whether it is inwardly motivated, as it ought to be, or imposed by necessity in a time of scarcity and rising prices, it is ethically and aesthetically correct and ecologically sound. Properly implemented, made a focal point in our way of life, it allows us to grace our table with a good dinner each day, reduce significantly its cost, and promote our effort to live appropriately, in harmony with Nature. Nor is this a utopian something-or-other, attractive in theory, a Sabbath piety that must yield to the realities of Monday morning. On the contrary, it is practical, realistic, and within the competence of anyone who is willing to make the effort.

In dealing with the second of these imperatives, I have no intention whatever of writing a conventional cookbook, of which there are already too many, most of which, in whatever category, do not differ enough from their predecessors to warrant publication. Examine with care, for example, the standard books on Italian and French cuisine. Note the recipes for veal scaloppine in the ones and for coq au vin in the others. Compare them in whatever other way, and convince yourself that the differences are not substantial. One may, of course, collect cookbooks as one collects stamps; but such a collection, per se, has little or no relevance to quality of the collector's cuisine.

I write this on the assumption that the main concern of the cook in a household is the preparation of a good dinner each day, an assumption that seems to me entirely realistic. For breakfasts and lunches, others in the household— except small children—usually fend for themselves. But the cook who approaches the dinner hour with intelligence and imagination cannot, nor does he wish to, avoid concern. For the dinner hour in any well-ordered family is the day's culmination; and its focus is the dinner. It can and it ought to be made a gay, relaxing conclusion to the day's labor. And the cook can do much to make it such by providing a dinner that inspires comment, appreciation, wonder, gratitude. And why not a toast proposed by one of the happy diners? Therefore, in the context of these reflections on ecological scarcity, and the despairing rise in the cost of living, a phenomenon that may be with us indefinitely, my emphasis is on suggested strategies for achieving economy and quality in the kitchen, as reflected in the dinner.

I have nothing to suggest by way of desserts, what our nineteenth-century ancestors called "dainties"; for they are brought to the table when they are generally quite superfluous, "which is unsatisfactory if they are not eaten and likely to be pernicious if they are." At any rate, whoever does the cooking in the American home needs no instruction in the preparation of a simple dessert. My advice is that you learn to do without it. Take it or leave it.

However, I offer another suggestion and urge you to

abide by it: avoid reliance on cookbooks, and let your goal be the progressive development of your own cuisine. Toward this end I give you the benefit of my own experience; but you must remember that it is intended to be merely suggestions. Cookbooks tend to be tediously repetitive; and one who slavishly follows them to the letter will never explore one's own resources, one's own culinary individuality. Have on hand one of the best and most complete cookbooks. And here I would recommend Irma Rombauer's *Joy of Cooking*. It has in it everything one needs to know about the culinary art and household economy. The recipes are brief, clear, reliable. But even these should be used, where possible, as points of departure. Follow a given recipe to the letter to get the feel of the thing, so to speak. Then taste the result and contemplate the ways in which the recipe might be varied. In this way you will develop your own culinary methodology; and unlike the assembly-line laborer, you will eventually produce something that is largely your own.

And once again I remind you, those of you who are so situated that you can grow your own herbs and vegetables, of the relationship between your cuisine and the kitchen garden; for the garden becomes, as it has for me, a veritable arsenal of culinary suggestions. As you survey what you have grown, and come to know their individual and collective virtues, they suggest what use you may make of them on any given day to produce a good dinner. I know whereof I speak, for I have learned to listen to mine. And they have never disappointed me.

I have used the phrase "a good dinner"; and by this I mean one such as current usage would call gourmet food: a dish of prime ingredients prepared with the appropriate condiments and flavoring agents. For example: a lamb chop pan-fried in vegetable oil with nothing but salt and pepper is good. If one uses a bit of olive oil and butter, a sprig of fresh rosemary, a clove of garlic, and a dash of lemon juice, it will qualify as gourmet food. Its "secret" is a knowledge of herbs and other flavoring agents and how to use them.

Note an instance of how easily such good, inexpensive food may be prepared.

I awakened early on a Monday morning late in July and frowned on the overcast that had been predicted. June and the first two weeks of July had been wetter and colder than normal and my dozen tomato plants, for lack of sun, were a fruitless mass of luxuriant foliage. Somewhat relieved by the weatherman's promise of sun later in the day, I had a light breakfast of toasted homemade bread, a bowl of raspberries taken from the garden, a cup of coffee laced with brandy; scanned the morning paper's gloomy news, skipped its daily stock of trivia, and went to my office to tend to my professional duties. By midafternoon, my day's quota of brain labor done, I went home to do some urgent work in the garden. The sun, as promised, had by now burned off the overcast; and the time was right for harvesting the shallots and the garlic and preparing the vacated space for sowing rutabagas and a fourth crop of turnips. The labor entailed, restorative and refreshing after several hours at the desk, would give the appetite a necessary edge.

On the way home I stopped at the supermarket to shop for dinner. My wife and I have a domestic arrangement, initiated when the children were infants and which has worked so well for these many years. Since they were all breast-fed, it was agreed that I would prepare the daily dinner while she nursed them and tucked them in for the night. I did this with ease and pleasure, for I had brought to the marriage some experience in cooking and grocery shopping. Later, what had been merely expedient became a convenient and mutually satisfactory routine. And now, when we have guests for dinner, as we frequently do, we work together in the kitchen. On other days I prepare the dinner and do the necessary shopping for it. She tends to the staples and all other household necessities. The arrangement is a happy one. It leaves her free to pursue a variety of creative activities, while I am quite happy tending to our bellies "very carefully and very studiously." The phrase is Doctor Johnson's.

For the Monday dinner I had planned, all I needed to buy was meat for two. I chose extra-lean ground beef, a trifle more than half a pound. The price was a dollar and fifty-two cents. At five-thirty, my work in the garden completed, I went to the kitchen, taking with me three artichokes the size and shape of large lemons, and two medium-size beets with ample crests of purplish-green leaves. To add to the greens I cut a few leaves of chard. I trimmed and thoroughly washed the root sections and put them on to boil. Later I would add the greens. While these were cooking, I trimmed the artichokes as described in the preceding chapter, cut each into six longitudinal slices, and immersed them in cold water acidulated with the juice of half a lemon. This would preserve their bright, yellow-green color. When the beets were done but not overcooked, I drained them, cut the root portions into thin slices, and minced the leaves.

An appropriate condiment for this and other vegetables, such as boiled or steamed green beans, zucchini, or cauliflower, is a blend of olive oil and butter, with a few drops of lemon juice and a mince of basil when that is available. On this occasion I used partially degreased roast drippings with a dash of wine vinegar. These I always save when I roast properly seasoned pork, beef, or fowl. A chicken, for example, laved with olive oil and stuffed with garlic, parsley, onion, celery, and sage or rosemary, will yield, when roasted, as you may well imagine, a third of a cup or so of marvelously flavored drippings. Having such on hand, I heated them in a saucepan, stirred the beets therein, added the necessary salt and a grind of pepper, and removed the pan from the burner. Warmed later, they would be ready to serve.

I then prepared the ground beef for pan frying. In an appropriate skillet I put a tablespoon of olive oil. When it was smoking hot, I removed the skillet from the burner, dropped two finely minced cloves of garlic into the hot oil, gave the skillet a swirl, and set it aside to cool. There was enough fire in the hot oil to barely brown the garlic. Having placed the ground beef in a bowl, I poured the oil and garlic over it, added salt and pepper, mixed the whole thoroughly with my bare hands so that the flavoring agents and the meat would be completely amalgamated, and shaped the compound into four thinnish patties. They were now ready for frying in the skillet in which the garlic had been browned. The three artichokes, cut into eighteen wholly edible wedges, were ready to be coated with a light batter, which I promptly made by stirring a bit of flour into a beaten egg.

By six o'clock these preliminaries were completed. To fry the artichokes in a second nonstick skillet with enough oil to cover the bottom, and the patties in the first skillet with no more oil than had been mixed with the meat, would require but a few minutes. I sliced the homebaked bread, fetched a bottle of our 1975 Cabernet from the cellar and pulled the cork. Knowing that dinner is invariably ready soon after six, my wife was at the door by the time the preparations were completed. She promptly set the table while I poured the drink we occasionally have before dinner. She had been at a painting class and brought home a partially completed canvas which she placed on the mantle. We reviewed it critically while we sipped our drinks.

At about twenty past six I returned to the kitchen while she scanned the news in the evening paper and finished her bourbon and soda. I dredged the artichoke slices in the batter, browned them lightly on both sides, sprinkled them with salt, pepper, a few drops of lemon juice, and arranged them on a hot platter overlaid with absorbent paper. Meanwhile, the meat patties were cooking over moderate heat in the other skillet. They might have been broiled, but I preferred to do them in the skillet. Since there was practically no fat in the ground beef, the meat juice released in the cooking, flavored with the oil and garlic, would produce a thin delectable sauce. These operations were conducted simultaneously, so that patties and artichokes were done at the same time. The beets had been kept warm in the saucepan.

At six-thirty I arranged the food in two equal portions on hot plates and called the mistress to dinner. We klinked glasses by way of grace and enjoyed our dinner in virtual silence, in deference to Beethoven and the Quartetto Italiano, who provided the dinner music.

You must have noted that the cost of the Monday breakfast and dinner, in out-of-pocket money, was a dollar and fifty-two cents. If the bread and berries for breakfast, the beets, artichokes, bread and wine for dinner had been bought, the day's expenditure would have been no less than ten dollars. Berries, beets, and bread, at current prices, would have cost as much as the ground beef. The price of three artichokes, and of such quality as we would frown upon, is two dollars and ninety-seven cents. A bottle of wine, of which we drank only half, comparable to our 1975 Cabernet, would have cost no less than ten dollars. And is there any doubt about the excellence of the dinner? One of comparable quality, in any of the few restaurants that have the means to produce it, would have cost a minimum of forty dollars. The wine itself would have cost twenty. In this context, could the meaning of creative assault on scarcity be made more vivid and compelling?

And we might make it more so by varying the menu in this way: Instead of the beets, take from the garden sufficient romaine and arugula (rocket) for a huge salad. Substitute four eggs for the ground beef. Cut the artichoke wedges into thin slices. Using a nonstick skillet, sauté them in a bit of oil, together with a few shallots, a mince of parsley, and nepitella (calamint), an appropriate flavoring herb for artichokes, cardoons, and mushrooms. When these are done, arrange the whole so that you have an even surface in the skillet, and pour over it the eggs beaten with a heaping tablespoon of grated Parmesan cheese. Cook over moderate heat for a couple of minutes and place it under the broiler until the surface is a somewhat puffy golden color. Loosen it around the edges with a spatula, slide it onto a hot platter, cut it in quarters as you would a pie. Serve it with toasted bread, buttered if you must, rubbed with garlic. Klink glasses by way of grace, and damn the brutal realities of inflation! Your out-of-pocket money is the cost of the four eggs. In celebration thereof, pour yourself another glass of wine.

And while you are in the euphoric mood, why not finish off the entire bottle in celebration of another discovery you have made: the inherent relation between an excellent cuisine and the kitchen garden? For if you grant, as you must, that you have eaten very well, as well, I dare say, as any educated palate requires and deserves, the virtue is in that "commodious and fair garden." Commodious for its convenience; for on any given day you may take from it what you need at the very moment that you need it. And the more so when what you require—an artichoke, a witloof chicory, a Savoy cabbage—may not be available at the market. And fair for the absolute freshness and integrity of its produce and its variety of such aromatic herbs as enhance the flavor of so many dishes—chives and parsley in an omelet, rosemary in pan-fried lamb chops, a combination of herbs in a good broth. Thus it may be fairly stated that an adequate kitchen garden makes possible a superior dinner each day.

And one that may be prepared rather quickly. There is

a mistaken notion abroad that a fine cuisine is a tediously laborious cuisine. Not so, generally. Some excellent dinners do require several hours to complete. I cannot, for all my experience and dexterity in the kitchen, make pasta and the meat sauce as a condiment for it, in less than two and a half hours; nor a dish of tripe in less than the hour necessary to prepare it for the oven and the four hours required to cook it properly. However, given the fair garden, the skill in the mechanics of cooking which one acquires with experience, a pantry well stocked with the necessary staples, and adequate kitchen utensils, a daily dinner of excellent quality can be prepared in about one hour. In the dinner described above I have indicated, step by step, how this can be done. Had I chosen to roast a frying chicken instead of serving the ground beef patties, it might have taken only a few minutes more.

But the few minutes more or less are of no consequence; what matters is the propriety, the adequacy of the time allotted each day for the routine preparation of dinner. My suggestion of an hour is not arbitrary; it is the result of many years in the kitchen. Vary it if you will. And what matters further is the ease, the leisurely pace, the very pleasure with which what was planned is executed. The facility is acquired by experience—experience informed by an undeviating adherence to the principle that every dinner must please an educated palate and provide the body its proper nourishment. Of the five senses, the sense of taste is the last to yield, undiminished, to the process of aging and decay. When one is well into the twilight years, one may not hear so well nor see so clearly; but if in reasonably good health, one's delight in a fine dinner will

be unimpaired. Hence the enduring importance of gastronomy as a constituent in a people's culture, and especially in
the cultures of France and Italy. Other people, too, have
their appropriate cuisine—the Jews, the Russians, the
Orientals, for example; and while I recognize their excellence, I give them here no more than a toast of praise for
the reason that, in this context, I am concerned only with
what is collectively called the "continental cuisine," that of
the southern portion of the continent of Europe.

The word "cuisine" derives from the Latin *coquina,*
kitchen. In France the word *cuisine,* and in Italy its equivalent, *cucina,* have a double meaning: the room in the home
where food is prepared for the table, and the characteristic
manner, the style, of preparing it. In English, "cuisine" has
only the second of the two meanings; for the first, we have
the familiar word "kitchen." This derives immediately
from the Middle English *kichene,* and ultimately from the
West Germanic *kocina.* The word "cuisine" we have
adopted from the French. Does this gap in the English language, and the fact that we have filled the gap by borrow-
ing from the French, suggest that America had no accomplished gastronomy; and that such gastronomy as we are
now intent on cultivating will be Mediterranean grafted
onto Nordic stock? The fact that during the past several
decades we have borrowed so lavishly, both from the culinary lexicon and the cookery of France and Italy, would
seem to suggest an affirmative answer to the question.

The cuisine of a people, what they eat and how they
prepare it, reflects, obviously and closely, their total environment—the climate, the land and its produce, meager or
prodigal, the edible resources of its waters. Less obviously

but no less closely, it also reflects their mode of life, their ethic, what they conceive to be the absolutely right and proper conduct of life. The cuisine of America before the first world war, found so inadequate by emigrants from southern Europe, conformed perfectly to these generalizations: It reflected the fairyland abundance of the New Land and the austere ethic of the early Anglo-Saxon settlers.

The abundance, however, lacked variety. It was limited to what I call the hard-core basics in every category of edibles: the most common produce, the most common flesh, fish, and fowl, the most common staples. We were there, my family and I, puzzled by the lack of all such ingredients as an accomplished cook needed to vary the menu and enhance the flavor of raw materials. Men and women now in their thirties can have no idea of the vast difference, in the variety offered, between the grocery store then and the supermarket now. (In order to have what was lacking, the immigrants settled in ethnic enclaves, established food stores, and imported what they needed.)

The native cuisine also lacked variety; it was bland. It had enormous body and little soul. I pay my respects to what Americans did very well—the southern-fried chicken, for example, and their breakfast, their manner of breaking fast and facing the day's labor with the human power plant stoked with pancakes, sausage, ham, bacon, chops, fried potatoes; and with such luxuries as quantities of cream, sugar, coffee. We immigrants, who then worked with pick and shovel ten hours a day, having learned from the natives how to prepare for it, added their breakfast to our daily menu. Quantitatively and qualitatively, that element in their cuisine was inspired. And there were, of course, pockets of culinary excellence, such as in New Orleans. Furthermore, the very rich, with ample means to travel and to import from abroad both cooks and what they needed for a "grand cuisine," dined as well as their peers in Europe. But mainstreet America neither had nor cared for anything beyond what has been rather loosely described as a meat-and-potatoes diet.

Puzzled at first by such a bland, limited cuisine, I learned later, as a student of American history, the reason for it. Its sobriety, the lack in it, beyond nourishment, of what is pure pleasure, reflected the austere ethic of the early Anglo-Saxon settlers. In that somber view of life, the Puritan ethic, all that contributed to purely sensuous pleasure, such as a glass of wine and pleasantly seasoned food, all that urged one to abandon Calvin and follow Epicurus and seek a measure of redemption in joyous living, was severely censored. A dish that smelled good and tasted even better than it smelled, and so was eaten with fresh appetite and heightened pleasure, would certainly stimulate appetites of another sort and urge one on to pleasures more visceral, especially if the "spicy" food were accompanied by a glass of wine. And that would spell damnation. So boil the potatoes, cook the meat without erotically stimulating seasonings, fill the dinner goblets with water, and let each one rejoice in the austere pursuit of business, the work ethic.

It was a cruel ethic, rooted in the asceticism of the Middle Ages, and sanctioned by a misreading of the Sacred Book. It achieved its highest eminence during the reign of Queen Victoria, and came to be known as Victorianism, defined by the *American Heritage Dictionary* as a doctrine of "moral severity or hypocrisy, middle-class stuffiness, and pompous conservatism." Its ruling apostles attempted to legislate out of existence certain wholesome appetites of the flesh, man's instinctive search for those experiences that yield immediate pleasures. And, in the long pull, it failed.

The effective revolt against pious pretensions and hypocrisies began in the early years of this century with the social criticism of such writers as Jack London, Upton Sinclair, Theodore Dreiser; and it gained momentum at the end of the first world war. London's book, *Revolution*, declared its intention in the title. In *A Preface to Morals*, Walter Lippmann condemned the old order with an impressive bill of particulars, and proposed in its stead the Religion of the Spirit. But as the revolt related to the art of living and the aesthetics of the table, the most engaging voices were the artists and aesthetes themselves, such literary worthies as Amy Lowell, Sara Teasdale, Sherwood Anderson, Edgar Lee Masters, and Edna St. Vincent Millay. A pervasive theme of their works was a cry for the liberation of the human spirit from the stranglehold of Puritanism, and a celebration of all that was censored by the Victorian ethic. And the flight of the artists of the "Lost Generation" (Gertrude Stein's description) was a symbolic affirmation of that passionately sought freedom. United in the conviction that in crude, materialistic America artistic creation was impossible, that band of talented writers sought inspiration in the warm glow of the uninhibited, uncensored Latin Quarter on the south bank of the Seine. And when they returned, their palates educated in the cafés and bistros of Paris, and did their important work on native grounds, the moral and aesthetic climate in America was more congenial to their labors.

This advance in the emancipation of the human spirit from the severe constraints of Puritanism, and the excellence of the authentically American literature of the postwar era, was an important phase of what a French social critic called "America's coming of age." Another change, closely related, was the beginning of a nationwide interest in gastronomy. As an on-the-spot observer of the phenomenon, and now for many years active in promoting its fruition, I first became aware of it soon after the war, not in a metropolis, but in the lumber town on the Northwest frontier to which we had come when I was ten years of age. Whereas the natives then had scorned us and our cuisine and contemptuously referred to wine as "dago red," they now began to exhibit some respect for what they had maligned. And it was the young men who had returned from the war who were responsible for the incipient enlightenment. Having fought shoulder to shoulder with dagos and eaten Italian food, they now spoke fondly of both and urged their mothers to learn from Mrs. Pellegrini how to make spaghetti. And thus it was that the tension between native and immigrant gave way to an increasingly friendly and mutually beneficial relationship. Mother was invited to join the Pythian sisterhood, for whom she cooked their occasional dinners; her eldest daughter was employed to cook for one of the lumber company's executives; her first grandson became the owner of the village supermarket, which he stocked with olive oil, Parmesan cheese, and other Italian staples. And since there were other Italian ladies skilled in the kitchen who were called upon to share their recipes, the cuisine of many a village household became Italianized. There is a touch of irony here.

I have recited this bit of personal and cultural history as it relates to the kitchen, noted the approximate beginnings of mainstreet America's interest in improving its cuisine and the spur given toward that end by its various immigrants, in order to place in historical perspective our current preoccupation with gourmet foodstuffs and gourmet cooking, an in-depth interest reflected in what a national weekly recently reviewed as a "cookbook craze." I have done this largely for the benefit of the young, who were not there to see what I have recorded, and as a necessary introduction to what I shall have further to say about the kitchen and the staff of life. And besides, is it not appropriate for every generation to be aware of the past as it relates to the present, and of both as they relate to the future?

Initiated in the early twenties, the main thrust toward the achievement of a superior cuisine came after the end of the second world war. For it was after the middle forties, during the boom decades immediately following Hiroshima, that the best of the current vast library of cookbooks and books on wine were published—classics by such professionals as Alexis Lichine, M.F.K. Fisher, James Beard, Michael Field, Roy Andries De Groot, Julia Child, Marcella Hazan. And I myself have contributed something to the gaiety of the dinner hour with my various publications and lectures during the past thirty years. Largely due to the salutary influence of these writers—and above all,

M. F. K. Fisher, the most literate and philosophical writer on gastronomy in America—there are now gourmet food sections in supermarkets, gourmet and wine columns in newspapers, gourmet restaurants and gourmet cooking schools in every city. There are wine and food societies, mycological societies, enological societies. And wine tastings are so much the "in" thing that even the W.C.T.U. must be reassessing the legitimacy of its ascetic goal. America seems hell-bent on achieving the highest culinary eminence. And she probably will, for we certainly have the will and the raw materials.

The effort and the accomplishment thus far must be applauded. But unfortunately, the most authoritative and widely read cookbooks are descriptive of what the French call the *haute cuisine*, high cooking, elaborate and expensive. Too many of the recipes, rigid, precise, elaborately described, give one the impression that only a master chef can properly execute them. Furthermore, when the procedure is slavishly followed, is the result appreciably superior in taste to what can be produced by methods more casual and less demanding? And again: the grand cuisine is a heavy, fat cuisine. So much so that the French who created it and so effectively promoted it in America seem to be having second thoughts about its salutary virtue. Several of their writers on food have been promoting what one of them calls the *cuisine minceur*, a "thinness," low-calorie cuisine. One hopes that such a revision of the classic style is based on sound culinary principles, and is not merely a public-relations thrust designed for export to weight-conscious and jogging America, where diet cookbooks are selling by the millions. In any case, regardless of motives, the revision is commendable.

However, a grand, classic, calorie-indifferent menu of several courses, each with its appropriate wine, has its proper place in any culture where the pleasures of the table are assiduously cultivated; but such a menu should be reserved for proportionately grand occasions, such as weddings, significant anniversaries, religious and secular festivals. Accordingly, every household should ritually celebrate its own select occasions with an appropriate feast, going to the masters, if need be, to choose from among their culinary triumphs such menus as best suit the family requirements. And it would be advisable on such occasions, as a part of the ritual itself, to have the entire family participate in choosing and executing the menus. This I would urge on both aesthetic and ethical grounds.

And here I am reminded of one of Doctor Samuel Johnson's happier asseverations: "I could write a better book about cookery than has ever been written: It should be a book upon philosophical principles." What an astute reflection upon the entire craft of cookery and cookbook writing! He did not, of course, mean that it would be what Sydney Smith imagined, a book on muffins and metaphysics, crumpets and logic. Nor, certainly, a pedestrian book of recipes. What he must have had in mind was a treatise on culinary philosophy, cuisine as it relates to civilized living; on the ethics and aesthetics of the entire process of planning, preparing, and eating a meal designed to nourish adequately the body and please completely an educated palate; on the enduring and ineffable delight with which one approaches the daily dinner; on a cultivated cuisine *in gremio familiae* as one of the most effective ways of strengthening family cohesion. And here I would urge you to give this observation its due attention at a time when the very young are taking to the street and the family is in jeopardy. For it is not stern exhortations and lip-service pieties that keep the traditional family intact, but rather a sensibly hedonistic approach to life, where the pleasures of the body and the pleasures of the mind are cultivated as a matter of course and kept more or less in balance. And of the various manifestations of such an approach, an exceptionally fine cuisine, sensed and appreciated by everyone and regarded as a family heritage to be passed on to the next generation, must surely be one of major importance.

It is some such cuisine, and so regarded, that I have been describing. Some such, I say, for there are other approaches that will yield the good results. However, in the context of these reflections on ecological scarcity and the despairing rise in the cost of living, my emphasis here is on suggested strategies for reducing the cost of a daily dinner of excellent quality. There is no attempt to describe such a cuisine in its entirety; and I am concerned only with the dinner. My hope is that the family cook will be inspired by what I suggest to preside over the kitchen with determination, economy, imagination; to abjure forever reliance on all species of prepared meals; to avoid as much as possible tinned and frozen edibles; and to prepare from scratch, day by day, such a dinner as will elicit from the entire family a heart-warming chorus of praise. It can be done; it can be easily and quickly done; it can be done with pleasure in the doing and enormous satisfaction in the results. Do I see you raising a skeptical brow? Must you have another demonstration by one no more endowed by Nature with culinary wizardry than you? Very well. You shall have it.

My wife, skilled in the kitchen—why dost thou think I married her forty-seven years ago?—attracted by a bottom round steak, the price of which had been inexplicably reduced from over five to a little more than two dollars, promptly bought it. (She has an eye for such bargains, even though she leaves the shopping for dinner to me.) I trimmed off all the fat and cooked it for Sunny, the family dog. What remained was pure, red beef, nicely marbled and well aged. (Was that age the reason for the reduction in price?) With half of it she made a favorite of hers, a very fine stew, which I supplemented with enough green beans from the garden to serve four people; for although we are two, we eat enormous quantities of vegetables.

The following day I cooked the other half in this way: I cut the meat into about three-inch squares, pounded them with the dull edge of the cleaver, dusted each with flour, and browned them on both sides in a bit of olive oil. It required but a few minutes. That done, I removed them from the skillet and sautéed therein, with no additional oil, six shallots, two cloves of garlic, a fistful of dry boletus mushrooms, a few sprigs of parsley and some celery leaves, all coarsely chopped. The mushrooms had been soaked in a cup of very hot broth. The meat was then arranged over the sautéed compound, half a glass of red wine poured over the whole, and the burner turned to high. When all was bubbling merrily and contrapuntally to my merry whistling and the wine reduced by half, I added the broth, in which the dry boletes had been soaked, jazzed up with a grind of pepper and a dash or two of Tabasco. No salt because there was enough of it in the broth. When the bubbling resumed, I lowered the heat; and when the liquid was partly reduced and the sauce nicely thickened by the flour with which the meat had been coated, I covered the skillet and left the amalgam to ripen for ingestion. The vegetable for that dinner was a large cauliflower, taken from the garden within the hour, steamed and made delectable with a condiment of roast drippings, lemon juice, and a sprinkling of grated Parmesan cheese. The entire operation required no more than an hour.

Note what was done with a piece of beef that cost a trifle more than two dollars. Had it cost twice the amount, the result, two fine dinners, would have been no less noteworthy. Note the quantity of the single cooked vegetable for each dinner. Note the time, the simplicity of the preparation, the scant use of fat. (You will assume, of course, and you will be right, adequate bread and fine wine, both produced in our home.) And you will note once again the inherent, the necessary, relation between a fine cuisine, the kitchen garden, and the cellar—remembering the proposed threefold creative assault on scarcity: Grow your own; cook your own; make your own wine.

Now then: Do you follow these culinary drolleries? Are you so awed by what I have described that you regard it as something beyond your competence? If so—but banish the thought! For I see the incipient smile, the glow of intelligence in your eyes; and I hear you say "How marvelously simple! How stupid of me not to have devised it myself! Why not try it immediately and perhaps vary the recipe in such and such a way? But the boletes—what are they?"

Let me tell you. They are various species of wild mushrooms. The best of them is *Boletus edulis,* called the King. Fresh, it ranks with truffles in excellence; dried, it is indispensable in the kitchen. And very expensive, forty or fifty dollars a pound. But don't despair. It and other edible and choice mushrooms are plentiful in the hills and meadows and lowlands of America. The trick is to find them. Get yourself a mushroom book and become a wily mushroom hunter. Wily's the word. Read my chapter in *The Savory Wild Mushroom*, published by the University of Washington Press. I have hunted wild mushrooms since I was a boy; and we now have a small fortune in dry boletes, enough to warrant their distribution in our wills. Had I bought the fistful used in the above recipe, the price would have equaled that of the meat. So, to vary the imperative, hunt your own; for man cannot grow boletes.

You will not find the above recipe, nor any of the others given thus far, in the cookbooks; for they are not taken from books on cookery. They derive from my variations on the regional cuisine of Tuscan Italy, a savory, balanced, rather lean cuisine, much more so than that of Bologna, which is unabashedly fat—*Bologna la grassa.* Some of my recipes have been, and continue to be, simply suggested by the culinary resources of my kitchen garden. They are not, then, strictly speaking, invented by me; hence, whatever virtue they may have derives from the original, which is Tuscan, and the variation, which is my own. One ingredient, frequently used, is our never-exhausted supply of wild mushrooms, some dried and others fresh, completely cooked for the table and then frozen. Another, seldom found in most kitchens, is capers preserved in salt rather than brine. Since you are not likely to find them even in the gourmet section of the super-market, try your luck at the Italian stores in San Francisco,

Boston, New York. Or, since technology has virtually reduced to zero the distance from here to there, get aboard the next flight to Florence, as I did not long ago, whence I returned with a supply of capers tucked in my tote bag, some of which I used yesterday when I cooked a couple of sea-run cutthroat trout. These had been lured from Puget Sound the day before. The silly things to mistake a baited silver spoon for a herring! But then, I have known sillier terrestrial organisms pompously and collectively known as *Homo sapiens.*

Have you a brace of such sea-run cutthroats or any other species of trout? Cook them partially in a couple of tablespoonsful, one of oil, the other of butter. Remove them from the skillet and put therein a mince of three shallots, two cloves of garlic, a dozen capers, a few sprigs of parsley, and a bit of *Mentha pulegium.* Stir the compound briefly over low heat, return the trout to the skillet, salt and pepper to taste, pour over the whole a sacramental spray of dry vermouth acidulated with the juice of half a lemon, increase the heat. And when the bubbling achieves a certain fury and the tempo of your whistling increases in anticipation, give the skillet two professional swirls, one to the left, one to the right, reduce the fire, clamp on the lid, and finish cooking the silly things. Pull the cork on a Robert Mondavi Fumé Blanc—it's the best of them all—call your mate to dinner, klink glasses by way of grace, take a ritual sip of the wine, give each other a knowing wink—it was my grandmother's silent praise of an exceptionally fine wine—taste the trout, and proceed to lick the platter clean.

The recipe is my variation of what is basically Tuscan

procedure. As I've mentioned, the cuisine of Tuscany, the region of which Florence is the center, is relatively lean, savory, and balanced. And here I am concerned with the *cucina casalinga*, home cookery, not that of the posh restaurants, but akin to that of the *trattoria*, the unpretentious family restaurant. The invariable balance consists of a first course—soup or pasta or rice—and a second of meat and vegetable, ordinary wine, and plenty of bread. When well done, and the exceptions are rare, that daily cuisine, like the provincial cuisine of France, is inexpensive, uncomplicated, and excellent. Its basic invariant, as in the recipe above, is a mince of appropriate flavoring agents. The Italian word for what I have thus far referred to as a mince is *soffritto*, or *battuto*, its synonym. It has a more precise culinary meaning than "a mince"; and there is no single-word equivalent for it in English. Since the distinction of so many dishes derives from it, an etymological note is in order.

The words derive from the infinitives *soffriggere* and *battere*, respectively. The one means to fry lightly; the other, to beat or pound. The dictionary definition of *soffritto* as a culinary term is "a *battuto* of onions, herbs, etc., lightly cooked in skillet or saucepan with oil, butter, or lard." *Battuto* is defined as a "compound of lard, meat, herbs, etc., used as a filling or condiment." Thus the words, frequently used interchangeably, mean substantially the same thing; however, a *soffritto* is not just a mince, but a certain kind of mince. The challenge, then, posed to every cook is to devise the appropriate *soffritto* for a given dish.

Other constants in the cuisine are tomato paste (known

in Tuscany as *conserva*), pancetta, and wine. The first is a staple and made in this way: Boil ripe or, better, overripe tomatoes when these are plentiful and inexpensive, in a large kettle with plenty of salt. Add enough parsley, celery leaves, and fresh basil for flavor. When thoroughly cooked, pour into a colander and drain whatever liquid flows out without exerting any pressure on the mass. The draining need not be complete. Press the residue through a Foley food mill—it will be quite runny. Place it in a shallow pan and reduce in a low oven until the consistency is approximately that of a light pancake batter, bearing in mind that the thicker it is, the less you use in a recipe. At this point, if there is plenty of hot sun, you can make *conserva* by drying it in the sun in shallow pans, stirring it occasionally, until it is of such consistency that it can be shaped into a ball with the hands. Pressed into small containers and overlaid with a thin layer of oil, it can be kept in the refrigerator indefinitely. The abundant salt, meaning somewhat too salty on the palate, serves as a preservative. Assuming a recipe for four or six people, an amount of *conserva* about the size of a cherry, dissolved in hot broth, will do wonders for a sauce which requires the flavor of tomato. Where drying in the sun is not possible, the sauce, heated to the boiling point, may be put up in sterile, hot half-pint jars without further processing. The aromatics cooked with the tomatoes make this far superior to the tomato sauce produced commercially.

Pancetta and wine, as flavoring agents, are other staples in the Italian kitchen. The name of the former derives from *pancia*, belly. That portion of the pig's belly whence slab bacon is derived, cured with salt, pepper, and spices, rolled tightly longitudinally, tied securely like a huge salami, is hung in a cool room for several months. When the cure is complete, it may be sliced thinly and

eaten as an accompaniment to bread or used as bacon. In cookery it is a basic ingredient in certain varieties of *battuto* used to flavor sauces, stews, and casseroles. Where it is not available, lean salt pork is a good substitute.

A *battuto* such as this, for example, makes an excellent sauce for pasta. Cut in thin slices a piece of pancetta or lean salt pork about the size of two thirds of a stick of butter. Using a kitchen cleaver or a chef's knife with a twelve-inch blade, reduce them to a paste on the cutting board. This is done by repeated taps with the sharp edge and folding over of the result. Mince finely four shallots, or an equivalent amount of onion, and a small rib of celery. Sauté together with the salt pork paste in a tablespoon of olive oil and one of butter over moderate heat. Then add a mince of three cloves of garlic, a few sprigs of parsley, and half a dozen leaves of fresh basil. Stir these thoroughly in the sauté and add immediately half a pint of your own tomato sauce diluted with half a cup of stock. If you must, substitute a small tin of the commercial product, or two large ripe tomatoes peeled and cut in small pieces. Add a dash of Tabasco, a pinch of allspice, one of nutmeg, pepper to taste, and simmer for about twenty minutes. The sauce will be adequate for twelve ounces of pasta, enough for four people. When it is served as a first course, two or three ounces of pasta per person are plenty; and it is advisable never to *drench* pasta with sauce. Keep the flavor subtle. A sprinkling of grated Parmesan on each serving is, of course, assumed. Note the leanness of the sauce, the blend of aromas, the inconsequential cost. A salad from the garden, balanced with a few slices of Monterey jack cheese would nicely complete a fine dinner.

One such, but different, I had last evening. I had just returned from a lecture engagement in Eastern Washington. Along the way, hungry and two hours away from home, I had stopped at one of those fast-food joints and ordered what had seemed relatively safe—a toasted Reuben sandwich, described as a combination of corned beef, sauerkraut, and cheese on rye bread. But what was served, flanked by a mound of limp, greasy, overcooked French fries of repulsive color, two thin, round slices of pickle, and a sprig of withered parsley, was a gooey desecration with a miserly slice of corned beef between two thin slices of soggy, greasy bread, and the whole sort of glued to a paper plate. Limp in the hand when I managed to extract it, this abomination contained a smear of mixed mayonnaise and kraut and I know not what pale cheese oozing and dripping from around the edges of the enfolding bread. And it wasn't toasted. It had been fried on a griddle smeared with stale grease, offensive to the nose and repugnant to the stomach. For on the way home, its inevitable regurgitations seemed to say "You fool! Why did you eat it?" Well! I was hungry. And the price was three precious dollars and ninety-five cents.

After several such reproachful regurgitations, I was at home near the dinner hour. What could I do by way of penance for a stomach not accustomed to such abuse, and to purge my system of the desecration I had ingested because I was hungry, abhor waste, had been served what I had ordered and paid dearly for it? Among the several options available and as an infallible restorative, I chose to make peace with my stomach by dining on *ribollito* and fresh figs. The word means boiled again. The ingredients are minestrone and stale bread. I had both on hand, having made a large kettle of minestrone a few days before and stored it in the refrigerator to mature. The figs, with a drop of honey at the base, a sure sign that they are ripe, were hanging along the boughs in our garden. I put the minestrone on the stove to reboil, and toasted several slices of homemade bread. When these were ready I rubbed them with fresh, juicy garlic, buttered them lightly and cut them into small squares. Then in a large bowl I alternated layers of bread and pourings of hot minestrone. When the bowl was filled to the brim, I set it aside long enough for the ingredients to marry and cool a little, while I went to fetch half a dozen figs. Now seated at the table I repeated an ancient ritual: *Pancia mia, fatti capanna*—O Belly of mine, make a storehouse of yourself—and slowly, methodically, gleefully ingested the whole. The stomach was now happy; and to add to its felicity, I gave it a glass of white wine. Then I sliced the figs, poured over them a bit of light cream, and ate them with gusto. Once again I suggest that you consider the inconsequential cost of such a salutary supper.

Its good taste and ample nutrients derive from the protein-rich minestrone made thus: In a soup kettle of six-quart capacity, cook one quart of shelled romani beans in two quarts of light stock. Lacking these, use a pound or more of navy beans. When thoroughly cooked, cream the beans by passing them through a food mill, using the liquid in which they were cooked to facilitate the creaming process. The result will be a thick bean broth. Using a chef's knife or sharp cleaver, mince to a paste a quarter of a pound of pancetta or lean salt pork. Add to the paste a large onion, a rib of celery, three cloves of garlic, six sprigs of parsley, and the leaves of a sprig of thyme, all finely chopped. Sauté all these ingredients in two tablespoons of olive oil over a slow fire, using the kettle in which the soup is to be made. Do not brown or burn. This is the appropriate *battuto*. Add two large peeled ripe tomatoes, or their equivalent of tomato sauce, *conserva*, or canned tomatoes, and a cup of stock. Simmer the whole for ten or fifteen minutes. This is the sauce, the important flavoring agent for minestrone. It must be thickly fluid, so use whatever amount of stock is necessary. Sprinkle generously with black pepper.

Dice a large carrot, a potato, four ribs of celery, and

braise in the sauce. While these are simmering, chop coarsely half a Savoy or other cabbage, a few leaves of curly kale and chard, one large zucchini squash. Add these, stir the whole thoroughly, cover the kettle, and braise gently for ten or so minutes. The braising cooks the flavor into the vegetables. Now add the bean broth and as much stock as necessary to produce a thick but fluid soup. (Minestrone is the Italian word for big soup.) Bring to a boil, taste for salt, reduce the heat, and simmer for about an hour. A few minutes before serving, stir in a cup of minced basil. If you like rice or pasta in your minestrone, cook whichever you like separately, about a third of a cup per person when cooked, drain, and add to the soup at the same time as the basil. Instead of these you may prefer the minestrone ladled over a slice of toasted homemade bread lightly rubbed with garlic. The final touch is a sprinkling of grated Parmesan cheese.

Quick-frozen minestrone may be kept for as long as a year without deterioration in quality. It is advisable, therefore, to make large quantities of it when herbs and vegetables are plentiful in the garden and at their best. Or you might simply freeze the vegetables, braised as directed, and have them on hand. The bean broth can be made as needed. Since a dinner of minestrone satisfies both body and soul, and its cost is minimal, even to one who has no kitchen garden, little else is needed—perhaps some fruit and cheese—to complete it.

There are numerous variants of this dish, called *zuppe,* plural of *zuppa,* in the *cucina casalinga* of Tuscany. They are all amalgams of various vegetables, the liquid in which they were cooked—either water or, preferably, a light stock—and toasted stale bread. They are thick, the scant liquid in which the vegetables were cooked being nearly all absorbed by the bread. One such, and a very good one, is made with cauliflower. Cut it in small pieces, including the inner, tender leaves, cook it in just enough stock, give it a generous condiment of olive oil, a mince of parsley and basil, appropriate salt and pepper, and pour it over the toasted bread rubbed with garlic. Hearty, nourishing, good and inexpensive, a dinner of such *zuppe* needs little else to round it out.

A suggested version of tarragon chicken for six, flavored with an appropriate *soffritto,* will not be much more expensive. Two young fryers will cost about four dollars. Bone them completely. If you have never performed this kitchen surgery, remember that quite ordinary people do it with ease. Simply cut and tear the flesh off the bones. With a little practice you will develop your own orthopedic technique. Put the bones, including the neck and wing tips, in a saucepan with two cups of water, a bay leaf, some onion, parsley, and leaves of celery. Bring to a boil and simmer long enough to reduce the liquid by half. Meanwhile, cut the meat in small pieces, discard the loose fat, dust the pieces with flour, and brown them in a combination of olive oil and butter, no more than necessary to coat the bottom of the skillet. When nicely browned on both sides, remove them with a slotted spoon. Now prepare a *soffritto* in that same skillet, with no additional fat, thus: Mince and sauté six shallots, three cloves of garlic, and a small rib of celery. Do this over low heat in order to avoid going beyond the required transparency in the ingredients. Now stir in a finely minced tablespoon of parsley and one of fresh tarragon. Sprinkle immediately over the whole a teaspoon of arrowroot for thickening. Stir with a spatula, add a scant glass of dry vermouth or white wine and a dash of Tabasco for piquancy. Increase the heat until the wine is partially reduced. Add the cup of broth made with the bones. Salt and pepper to taste, and finish cooking the chicken in the sauce over moderate heat. Do not overcook. A slow half-hour's simmering in the covered skillet should be enough. With plenty of bread from your oven, a salad from the garden, and a bottle or two of wine from your cellar . . . What else dost thou need to say you have dined well?

The above is an account of one use of the flavoring agent known as *soffritto*. One immediately thinks, or should think, of ways to vary it, using mushrooms, fresh or dried, tomato sauce, and an herb other than tarragon as the presiding aromatic. And does it not also suggest the use of such a *soffritto* to give stews or sautés of veal, lamb, and beef such gustatory distinction as will elicit the familiar chorus of praise—bearing in mind, of course, that sage is appropriate for veal, rosemary for lamb, and mushrooms for all, especially the dry boletes for beef? Suggests is the word; for a determined cook, intent on economy and learning, will always be on the alert for possible variations on a given culinary theme.

The Staff of Life

And now a concluding note on bread as the staff of life. I have already noted that America is well on the way toward achieving a certain culinary eminence; and yet there is a regrettable gap in its gastronomic coming of age.

For what is missing is a nationwide appreciation for what is historically called the staff of life, bread that crackles and sings in the mouth and that needs neither butter nor jam nor any other spread to make it palatable. We have borrowed lavishly from the cuisine of the French, less of the Italians, but we have learned little or nothing from the French *boulanger* and the Italian *fornaio,* bakers of bread exclusively and respected as such. For in those countries bread is the indispensable half, or more, among the poor, of every meal, gourmet or otherwise.

Years ago a French film was released that dramatized the primacy of bread in every community. The wife of the village baker took to the hills with a shepherd of notorious virility. The reaction of the villagers, especially the men, was characteristically French. They winked wickedly to each other, with a toss of the head toward the *boulangerie,* making simultaneously the sign of cuckoldry with upthrust index and little finger. However, when the grief of the humiliated baker was reflected in the bread, variously burned or underdone or not baked at all, the shoe was on the other foot. A town meeting was called, a search party organized, and righteousness triumphed. Thereafter the baker had his wife, and the villagers their bread. Supposing the wife of the president of an American baking combine were to take to the Bahamas with the president of a steel corporation, would the grief of the husband be reflected in the deterioration of what issued from this mechanized ovens? Could any such thing be possible? Banish the thought!

Some months ago there came to our city from New York a famous restaurant critic to review a dinner served in a certain gourmet restaurant. His published evaluation required half a page of a daily newspaper. The bread was not even mentioned. Strange omission! And yet, not so strange. For the quality supermarket that takes pride in its wine list, its gourmet food section, its royal cuts of meat for gourmet eating, lacks the necessary bread section to complete the gastronomic circle. What passes for bread is a puffed-up desecration wrapped in cellophane. Years ago it was scourged by the vitriolic pen of the archconservative columnist Westbrook Pegler, and more recently by the equally vitriolic pen of Henry Miller. And there I shall let the matter rest, for I am more at home in the constructive mood.

Therefore, let us explore the possibility of baking bread in the home. Professional moralists maintain that institutions cannot be changed without first changing the hearts of men. Similarly, I would say that mainstreet America will insist on authentic bread only when it has learned what the French and Italians and other Europeans have known from time immemorial, that bread is an indispensable element in the good life. And here I have in mind especially the generation that is on the very threshold of founding families. I would urge them to accept bread for what it is, the staff of life, the mainstay of every meal, and to eat more of it. And I would urge this for aesthetic reasons as well as for reasons of economy. The fullness of the flavor of a sauce, of flesh fish or fowl, of a cheese is best realized on the palate only when every intake is masticated with a bite of genuine bread. This is not a whim, a prejudice of mine; it is the judgment of people who mind their bellies very carefully and very studiously. "Waiter, more bread, please!" is the familiar call of diners in the restaurants of France and Italy. And the more bread ingested at dinner, the less the quantity of its costly accompaniments —a six-ounce steak instead of one of twelve. And the best way to learn this new approach to bread is to bake your own.

Baking bread is not in the least difficult. If you should be inclined to doubt your competence, or to avoid the attempt because making bread is too laborious and time-consuming, bear in mind that the most ordinary people in the world have been doing it for centuries with dispatch and utmost ease. True enough, the time required from the mixing bowl to the baked loaf is about five hours; but the labor involved will not be much more than thirty minutes once you have mastered the elementary mechanics. So get on with it, for even your first partial success will be much better than the cellophane-wrapped desecration.

I use that disparaging word "desecration" advisedly, for it means the abuse of the sacredness of something. And when I was a young boy in Italy I was taught that bread was sacred. Therefore, if a piece were dropped, it was to be retrieved, brought to the mouth with a cruciform gesture and kissed. I have never had occasion to doubt what I was taught—even in excessively hygienic America, where a piece of bread accidentally dropped is immediately retrieved and thrown into the garbage pail; and where, while in elementary school, I silently reproached my companions who, when they ate their lunch of jam sandwiches and the usual cut of pie, always discarded the fringe of crust.

It is not possible to detail a recipe for bread and directions on how to do the necessary work such as will assure immediate mastery of the mechanics and success in producing the perfect loaf. The accounts I have read in fastidiously precise cookbooks, accompanied by illustrative drawings of the necessary manipulations, may be letter-perfect; but they give the impression that the baking of bread is much more difficult than it is in fact. What goes by the name of French bread, dinner bread as distinguished from the numerous variety breads, is made with hard-wheat flour, yeast, salt and water. There is no difficulty whatever in mixing the ingredients in an appropriate container. What requires some skill is kneading the dough until it is just right and shaping the loaves. And this one must learn by doing. I cannot, nor can anyone else, put into meaningful words the feel and the appearance of the dough when properly kneaded, and the time required to do the job. I have learned to do the mixing and the kneading for half a dozen loaves in less than twenty minutes. Someone else, after a few trial runs, may do it in more or less time. Accordingly, I shall describe the entire process in sufficient detail to guide the novitiate in finding his own way.

You will need a large mixing bowl, metal or ceramic, about fourteen inches in diameter at the top; a large, sturdy wooden spoon for mixing; a smooth kneading surface about a yard square; a baker's metal scraper for scraping the sticky dough off the kneading board; a four-foot length of canvas pastry cloth about twenty inches wide; a cut of asbestos cement board an inch narrower than the oven rack; a razor blade and a small pastry brush. For four French loaves you will need three and a half cups of water, about seven and a half cups of unbleached flour, a tablespoon of salt, and a package of dry yeast.

With all these materials and equipment at hand, proceed thus: Pour the yeast in a cup of hot but not scalding water. In about five minutes the yeast will be activated. Meanwhile, put the rest of the warm water in the bowl, add the salt and about three cups of the flour. Stir vigorously for a few minutes, then stir in the activated yeast. Add more flour, a cup at a time, and continue the stirring. When the dough begins to thicken and stirring with the spoon becomes too difficult, and about three cups of the flour remain, discard the spoon and continue mixing with your hands. Work the flour into the sticky dough, a bit at a time, by pinching with both hands, turning the mass over, dusting the surface with flour, and punching it down with your fists. As it sticks to the sides of the bowl, dust the area with flour and press the adhering dough off with your fingers. Repeat this as often as necessary to keep the sides of the bowl clean. Rub your hands with flour from time to time to remove the sticky dough.

Bear in mind that what you seek to accomplish is a well-kneaded dough, smooth, elastic, and satiny, of such density that when a finger is thrust into it and quickly withdrawn it will come out clean—a mass that when held in the palm of the hand will slowly flatten out and droop at the edges. To achieve this, most of the kneading is done in the bowl by repeated punching with the fists, turning the mass over, and sprinkling its surface and the bottom of the bowl with driblets of flour until the dough no longer sticks to the bowl and hands. In order to avoid making the dough too dense, you should add the last cup of flour as needed and in driblets. When the kneading is nearly completed, give the dough a final turn on the kneading surface lightly dusted with flour. Roll it back and forth with the palms of the hands. When the roll is about twenty inches long, fold it so that the two ends are joined, using the scraper to lift it off the board. Repeat this a few times, then work it into a ball, rub it very lightly with a few drops of oil, return it to the bowl, flatten it, and spread a cloth over the bowl. Let it ferment slowly at room temperature. It will take about two hours, at which time the fermentation will have increased the bulk to about twice its size.

The forming of the loaves is a simple process. Deflate the leavened mass in the bowl by punching it down until it is flat. Put it on the kneading board dusted with flour and shape it into a roll about twenty inches long. Cut it into four equal parts. Let them rest for about ten minutes. Slap them briskly on the board for further deflation, then make of each a square measuring about five inches along the sides. Fold each square once, press the two edges together, and roll into a loaf about a foot long. Dust the canvas pastry cloth with flour, set the loaves on it in sequence, a tuck in the cloth separating each loaf from the other. Cover them with a cloth and let them rise for one hour.

Place the sheet of asbestos cement board on the oven rack with a small pan of hot water under it, and preheat the oven to four hundred. Have at hand a smooth wooden paddle six inches wide and two feet long. To put the loaves in the oven proceed thus: Dust the paddle with flour to prevent sticking. Place it parallel with a loaf, and with a deft upthrust of the cloth, turn the loaf upside down onto the paddle. Brush the loaf lightly with water and make two oblique slashes on it with the razor blade. To set the first loaf on the baking surface, align the paddle with one edge of the asbestos cement board and withdraw the paddle briskly. The loaf will easily glide off the flour-dusted paddle. Arrange the other three in the same way, being careful to leave an inch of space between them. Reduce the oven temperature to three-fifty after the first half hour. At the end of an hour the bread should be properly baked. However, it is advisable to inspect it after forty-five or fifty minutes. If the bottom is light brown and tapping it with the finger tips produces a distinct hollow sound, the baking is completed.

Such is the way I bake our bread. Solid, substantial, full of flavor, it resists pleasantly, as authentic bread ought, the muscular bite. Follow the directions and learn by doing. Nor must you forget while you work the joy implicit in what you are doing. Therefore, whistle merrily, smile broadly, hum a tune; for in having bread, man, you are among God's chosen people! And the cost of the four loaves? Less than the price of one cellophane-wrapped desecration.

The time required for the rising of the kneaded dough, technically the fermenting process, varies according to room temperature and the efficacy of the yeast. Given a good yeast, the dough will·ferment, slowly of course, even in the refrigerator. The time I have indicated is approximate and intended to give you an idea of the total time required to bake a few loaves of bread. Therefore remember two things: The kneaded dough is properly fermented when the generated gas gives it the appearance of about double its unleavened mass. As to the loaf: its final enlargement must be effected soon after it is placed in the oven. In order for this to happen it must be put in while the fermentation is still in progress; for if the fermentation is completed, the loaf, having no gas in it to make it rise, will fall. Hence, keep an eye on it; and when the dough is about half again as large as when first formed, put it in the oven and hope for the best. Once again I repeat: One learns by trial and error.

And now a concluding suggestion. If you have followed me eagerly and joyfully thus far, you are entitled to know the fullness of joy by going a step further. When I bake bread I occasionally make a few rosemary rolls and always some variant of pizza. Pizza was a creation of the Neapolitan housewife. The original, now varied in so many ways, was a leavened bread dough rolled into disks or rectangles about a third of an inch thick and overlaid with anchovies and slices of mozzarella cheese and tomatoes. In Tuscany and elsewhere north of Naples, the same thing, but with a more simple dressing, is called *schiacciata* (*sch* has the sound of *sk*). The name is the past participle of *schiacciare,* which means to crush or flatten. Another name for it is *focaccia.*

When the loaves are formed, reserve a part of the dough, enough, let us say, to make a rectangle more or less the size of a cookie sheet when rolled a third of an inch thick. The rolling should be done on the cookie sheet on which the *schiacciata* will be baked. Brush the surface with olive oil, sprinkle it with salt and pepper, and bake it in an oven preheated to three seventy-five degrees. When it is lightly browned on both sides—in about thirty minutes—it will be done, and by that time the loaves will be ready for baking.

Such was the way my mother made *schiacciata* in Italy,

and we ate it in lieu of bread on the day it was made. My own variation, which I shall make, at his request, for Fred Brack, my journalistic colleague, on his birthday two days hence, is done in this way: When the dough is rolled out, I brush the surface generously with olive oil and, what my mother lacked in the old country, melted butter. Then I scatter over the whole finely minced garlic and rosemary leaves, enough so that the entire surface is dotted with these aromatics, plus a sprinkling of salt and lemon pepper. As to the amount of garlic: Let it be enough so that the next day your exhalations will purge the air that enfolds you of all its impurities.

The rosemary hard rolls, so far as I know, are strictly Florentine. Take a handful of dough, roll it into a disk, scatter the surface with minced rosemary, fold it, overspread it with more rosemary, fold it again and shape it into a roll. Let it rise for half an hour and bake it according to the directions given for bread.

I suggest that you learn to make bread, *schiacciata,* and rolls in such a sequence that when one is baked, the next is ready for the oven. Since the *schiacciata* needs no rising, that will go in the oven first. The other two should rise for about half an hour. Therefore, form the rolls at the same time that you roll the dough for the *schiacciata,* and the loaves at the same time that you put the rolls in the oven, after the *schiacciata* is baked. If you bake the three in this sequence, the oven is used continuously and there will be no need for reheating it each time.

I have given you the best of what I know toward the making of bread as a creative and festive occasion; and I can assure you that your efforts will be appreciated and applauded by those for whom you bake. A few days ago I received a letter from Maya, our thirteen-year-old grand-daughter in Philadelphia. It dealt in part with her mother, Toni, making bread, and that "marvelous *schiacciata*" she had learned to bake in our home. Need I say more? Urge the obvious? Perhaps only this: Henry Adams, reflecting on his years at Harvard as a professor of history, stated that "a teacher affects eternity; he never knows where his influences will stop." We are all teachers at times and in various ways. Let us bear this in mind, and transmit to our posterity the best of what we know about the art of living. There is no more congenial way to firm the intergenerational bond.

Our granddaughter Sarah Owens is now eighteen. She is anxious to learn from her mother, Angela, and from us, the fundamentals of the culinary art. Her request to be taught simply reflects her own sense of the value of what she has enjoyed at the dinner table. And we have every reason to believe that Maya and Sarah will pass on what they have learned. The ghost of Henry Adams will smile approval.

Some Further Culinary Themes

I have used the word "themes" for this section rather than "recipes" because my intent is to awaken culinary inventiveness by proposing points of departure, rather than absolutes to be followed to the letter. Thus, while I shall be explicit and precise in describing how certain raw materials are converted into savory fare for the table, the implication will always be that what I propose may be varied in whatever way promises to please one's gustatory fancy. Given prime raw material, the excellence of a dish is always the function of the flavoring agents used in its preparation. And since these are many and varied, what pleases one may not necessarily please another. For example: Does a bit of curry and crushed garlic improve for you, as it does for me, an oil and vinegar dressing for salad? But for one whose experience in the kitchen is limited, a variation is best tried after one has followed closely the suggested recipe.

Pasta is now an Italian word firmed in the culinary lexicon of America. There are machines for making it in the home, fresh pasta shops in shopping malls, and the finest dry pasta imported from Italy in supermarkets. What cannot be bought in America is the variety of sauces used in dressing pasta. What can be bought as "spaghetti sauce," even that made by Italian enterprisers, is mentioned here only to warn you to avoid it.

There are many sauces for pasta; and you may properly want to add to the list. The simplest is a dressing of olive oil or butter or a blend of the two, in whatever quantity satisfies your taste. Mix the pasta thoroughly with the condiment and sprinkle each serving lightly with grated Parmesan cheese and, if desired, a bit of lemon pepper. There is no specific required amount of these flavoring agents. One must simply proceed according to one's taste, bearing in mind that, whatever the sauce, the pasta ought not to be drenched with it. As already noted, keep the flavor subtle; don't smother the pasta with an excess of condiment.

This simple sauce may be varied in these ways: Add to the oil and butter a mince of several cloves of garlic and a tablespoon of minced parsley lightly sautéed, being careful not to burn them. Or, for an exceptionally appetizing and piquant sauce for one pound of pasta proceed thus: In half of a quarter-pound stick of butter and a tablespoon of olive oil, sauté very lightly a mince of six cloves of garlic and eight filets of anchovies. Add an eight-ounce tin of tomato sauce—Hunt's, preferably—diluted with a third of a cup of dry vermouth or white wine and a dash of Tabasco, and simmer for a few minutes. The result will make you wonder how you managed to live without it for so long.

Three or four ounces of uncooked pasta yield a generous individual serving. The proportions in the above and all recipes hereafter are adequate for a dinner for four. There are three seafood sauces for pasta that deserve to be more widely known: clam, crab, and shrimp. The herbal basis for all of them is the same. In the half of a quarter pound of butter and tablespoon of oil mince and sauté four shallots or green onions. When these attain the proper transparency, add three cloves of garlic, finely minced, and a tablespoon each of minced parsley and celery leaves. If you have it in your garden, add a teaspoon of *Mentha pulegium*—English pennyroyal. Give the saucepan a stir and add immediately an eight-ounce tin of tomato sauce and the juice of half a lemon. Salt and pepper to taste, simmer briefly, and then add a cup of the chosen seafood. Bring the sauce to a low boil, cover the pan and turn off the burner.

All these sauces are simple, tasty, and easily prepared in just a few minutes. So is the triumph of northern Italian cuisine known as *pesto*. The name derives from *pestare*, which means to crush—in this case with a mortar and pestle, although this tool of the apothecary is not strictly necessary. For a pound of pasta, heat a quarter pound of butter and add thereto a loosely filled cup of fresh basil leaves minced with six cloves of garlic and a tablespoon of crushed pine nuts. If you don't have pine nuts, substitute raw almonds. If you are indifferent to calories, and your mechanism requires a lot of lubricating butter, use more than specified and tell your doctor to mind his own business. But remember that drenching pasta with sauce is the way of gluttons, not of discriminating eaters; and that the post-mortem future of gluttons is a circular area in hell plagued by an eternal storm of heavy hail, foul water, and snow. This on the authority of Dante, who visited the place seven centuries ago.

And Dante knew a thing or two about civilized dining, for he lived in Florence, in the heart of Tuscany, where one may find the classic meat sauce for pasta. Since I too was born in Tuscany, here is my version of that sauce. Cut into thin slices and then into tiny cubelets about the size of peas, a quarter of a pound of round steak and a slice of partly lean salt pork equal more or less to a slice of bacon. Dice similarly the gizzard and liver of a chicken. (Why not have pasta as an accompaniment to fried chicken?) Mince very fine half a medium onion, four cloves of garlic, and six fresh mushrooms. Combine these with the meat and sauté in three tablespoons of olive oil. In order to sauté properly, use a saucepan the bottom of which is no less than eight inches in diameter. Stir frequently over medium heat until all the meat is of a light-brown color. Then add, finely minced, a tablespoon of parsley, one of celery, and a teaspoon each of fresh sage, thyme, and rosemary. Stir them thoroughly into the sauté and then add immediately an eight-ounce tin of tomato sauce and an equal amount of beef or chicken broth. Increase the heat until the sauce begins to bubble, then lower it enough to effect an easy simmer. Stir to prevent sticking, and as the sauce reduces, add driblets of red wine to keep it dense but fluid. Half an hour of simmering will be enough. Now adjust it for salt and pepper, add a shake of allspice, one of nutmeg, and the rind of half a fresh lemon, finely minced. Stir well and continue the simmer for a few minutes. Such is the incomparable meat and herb sauce for pasta; and it can be easily prepared in less than an hour. Remember, this is enough for one pound of pasta.

A word now about the proper way to cook pasta. Use a large kettle, four- or five-quart capacity, for one pound of any sort of pasta. Give the pasta plenty of room to roil and roll; otherwise the strands will stick together. Drop it slowly in boiling salted water, a bit at a time, so that the boiling is never appreciably decreased. Cook it *al dente*, which is the Italian way of saying don't overcook. Have ready and very warm a large mixing bowl. When the pasta is done, strain it in a colander, shaking it vigorously to get rid of all the water; then pour over it boiling water, and rotate and shake the colander briskly once more. This will wash off all the excess starchiness so that, when served, the pasta will not be a sticky mess. Continue the rotating and shaking as you transfer it from the colander to the heated mixing bowl and pour the sauce over it immediately. Using a large serving spoon and fork, mix the pasta and sauce thoroughly as you would toss a salad. This procedure and the fluid sauce will prevent the stickiness you want to avoid. Serve promptly on hot plates in portions appropriate to each diner's capacity, and pass the grated cheese so that each may sprinkle as much as he or she requires. However, a word of warning is in order: Too much cheese will destroy the flavor balance.

Pasta being Italy's contribution to the cuisine of the Western World, it is appropriate to note that Italians, when they dine, serve it as a first course, so that it may be enjoyed, with whatever sauce, for what it is in itself. It may, however, be served in lieu of potatoes or rice as an adjunct to the main course. But this, though at times expedient, is not advisable. The taste, as pure sensory pleasure, of various sauces—especially of such as pesto and that marvelous anchovy sauce—should not be confounded on the palate with that of anything else. May I then suggest that you follow this procedure: Enjoy your pasta, drink a glass of white wine, be aware of your blessedness, compliment the cook, and proceed with the main course. What shall it be? A roast of chicken, pork, beef, lamb? These may be prepared for the oven in these ways.

Beef: make in it several deep incisions on both sides. Put therein salt, pepper, half a clove of garlic, and a few drops of olive oil. That is all. These flavoring agents will permeate the meat and give it a culinary transcendence. Do likewise to the pork but insert also a leaf of fresh sage in each incision.

Lamb: remove the bone and in the consequent cavity distribute rosemary leaves, chopped garlic, a dozen capers, the juice of half a lemon, salt, pepper, and a sprinkling of olive oil. Fit the bone back in the cavity, tie the meat securely, and the roast is ready for the oven.

Chicken: make a mince of garlic, parsley, celery, and sage leaves. Put the mince in a small bowl, add thereto two tablespoons of olive oil and one of wine vinegar. Lave the chicken inside and out with this mixture, salt and pepper to taste. Arrange over the breast of the chicken two slices of bacon, and it is ready for the oven.

When any of these roasts are sliced for serving, deglaze the roasting pan with half a glass of dry vermouth, and pour the resulting hot aromatized juice over the meat. "Transcendence" is the proper word to describe the quality these flavoring agents give to the roasts. You will note, of course, the relevance of the kitchen garden to these various culinary suggestions.

And now an all-purpose sauce for fish for four. In a pat of butter and two tablespoons of olive oil, sauté a mince of two shallots or green onions, two cloves of garlic, three sprigs of parsley, six capers, and enough English pennyroyal to make a minced teaspoon. Lacking this, use a leaf of sorrel. If you have neither, you have neglected the kitchen garden, which is regrettable, since you are not likely to find these herbs in the supermarket. Sauté the above briefly over a low fire. Avoid burning or browning. When done, set the mince aside while you poach a pound or so of cod, sole, salmon, or snapper in a small quantity of white wine or dry vermouth. When poached, transfer the fish to a container that can be placed under the broiler and set it aside. Stir in three quarters of a cup of the wine in which the fish was poached, a third of a teaspoon of arrowroot, and a tablespoon of lemon juice. Pour this over the sauté and reduce over low heat until the sauce is thickish but fluid. Salt and pepper the fish to taste, pour the sauce over it, and put it under the broiler until the sauce bubbles and the color is a very light brown. Serve immediately, repent your nastier sins, count your blessings, and *buon appetito.*

Serve with the fish potatoes done as follows. Peel and cut them in half lengthwise. Cut each half in three slices. Into a nonstick pan of adequate size, such as a shallow baking pan, pour enough olive oil to cover the bottom. Place it in an oven preheated to four hundred fifty. When the oil is smoking hot, throw in the potatoes and give the pan a vigorous shake so that each slice is immediately seared by the hot oil. The searing seals the surface of the potatoes so they will be crisp and coated but not soggy with oil. Be sure that each slice is entirely in the oil. (Hence the need for a pan of adequate size.) When this is done, assuming enough potatoes for four, scatter over them four coarsely chopped cloves of garlic and a heaping tablespoon of minced sage or rosemary or a combination of the two. Give the pan another vigorous shake so that the aromatics get into the oil and are properly distributed. Return the pan to the oven, and when the slices are nicely browned on one side, turn them over and sprinkle them with salt and pepper. When done to a golden brown, lift them onto absorbent paper with a slotted spoon and serve them immediately. If necessary they may be kept in a warm oven until ready to serve. But not for too long. The oil, now aromatized, may be kept for further use.

Potatoes thus prepared, so easily, so simply, with no possibility of failure, belong in the highest category of transcendence in the culinary art, a degree above such rare and expensive exotics as truffles. If, as is likely, you have never had them done this way before, either at home or at Sloppy Joe's or at a many-starred restaurant, don't curse yourself for the deprivation! Hell no! Call on the future to redeem the past. Where matters of the belly are at issue, wisdom enjoins regretting what one lacked yesterday and requires the fullest enjoyment of what is at hand. Grow your own tubers. Have them every day hereafter. However, a word of caution is in order. Potatoes prepared as here directed tend to promote gluttony; and I have warned you elsewhere, on the authority of Dante, about the post-mortem fate of gluttons. One can avoid it by being habitually prudent, a virtue which does not exclude—and here I think Dante as a genuine Florentine would agree—affirming one's humanity by an occasional overindulgence.

And here I am reminded of Father adding his own to the various Beatitudes recorded in the fifth chapter of the Gospel according to Matthew. In our new home in America, then blessed with an abundance of companatico, roasts were carved in the kitchen by Mother and brought to Father in the *vassoio,* a large serving platter. The Patriarch served himself, then passed the *vassoio* to his right, to me, his eldest son and heir according to primogeniture; and although there was plenty for all and more in reserve, he occasionally invoked the Cardinal Virtue, *Prudentia,* as he passed the *vassoio* through me to the rest: *Beati gli ultimi se i primi sono prudenti.* Blessed are the last if the first are prudent. It was his good-humored way of teaching us, by parable rather than heavy exhortation, to live appropriately. And since Catholics do not generally read the Bible, he was not thinking of the Beatitudes as he intoned the ritual words which, in substance, were in complete harmony with their presiding spirit. Being a wise peasant, a man of the soil, he was drawing on the collective wisdom of mankind, to which the lowly have contributed no less than the privileged since man began to think about the art of living.

And about household economy, which is the subject of these culinary suggestions for ways of eating well with due attention to proper nourishment and maximum pleasure in ingestion: No dinner or lunch conforms so well to these requirements as one of frittata and bread. *Frittata*, like the word *pasta*, is now generally incorporated in the culinary lexicon of America. It is a compound of vegetables, eggs, and cheese. It may be enriched by the addition of small amounts of bacon or bulk pork sausage. Since it is such a compound, there are as many frittate—plural of frittata—as the resourceful cook may devise. The vegetables most commonly used are spinach, chard, artichoke hearts, asparagus tips, potatoes combined with dry onions, leeks, and green onions, using of these last two both the white and green portions. The aromatics from the kitchen garden may be shallots, garlic, marjoram, parsley, basil, and tarragon. One may also use any desired combination of these. The recommended cheese is grated Parmesan. Where this is not available, shredded jack cheese is a good substitute. The recommended eggs are such as are dropped by hens who are enjoying a perfectly normal sex life with virile roosters in grubby barnyards. Lacking such, do the best you can with eggs dropped by flocks of virginal white leghorns, who may or may not be happy in coops where cock-a-doodle-doo is never heard.

In making frittate, the procedure is the same no matter

what ingredients are used. Bearing in mind that frittata and bread are to be the entire lunch or dinner, choose the vegetable base in whatever quantity seems adequate for the number to be served. Chop the vegetables coarsely and sauté them in oil or butter or bacon drippings in a nonstick skillet of such size as necessary for a frittata that will be about one inch thick when finished. Beat the eggs, one per person, in an appropriate bowl. Stir into them the grated cheese, at the rate of a heaping tablespoon for four eggs, and the same quantity of minced parsley or basil or tarragon or a combination of these, with adequate salt and pepper. These aromatics are merely suggestions, for if your kitchen garden is what it ought to be, there will be others available such as chervil, borage, oregano, marjoram, summer savory.

When the vegetable base is thoroughly cooked, remove the skillet from the burner and add the egg mixture. Stir sufficiently to combine the two, give the skillet a vigorous shake, and, with the aid of a spatula, effect an even, level surface. Place the skillet over low heat, shake it slowly, run the spatula around the circumference as the egg hardens and sticks to the edge of the skillet. When the bottom portion is done, place the skillet under the broiler until the surface is a puffy golden brown. Probe it with the tine of a fork to make sure the egg at the center has set. Now slide the finished frittata onto a serving platter; admire it; compliment yourself; cut it into equal portions; and with a silent prayer of thanksgiving, bring it to the table.

As already noted, a frittata may be enriched in taste and nourishment by adding bulk sausage or bits of crisp bacon to the vegetable base. Whether the one or the other is used, cook it first to get rid of the fat. Crumble the sausage as it cooks. For a final touch of elegance—and why not?—inlay the surface of the frittata with very thin slices of Italian salami or prosciutto before putting it under the broiler.

I have described the making of a frittata in some detail because it is the very prototype of household economy. Inexpensive, it conforms to the requirements of every civilized dinner: balance, complete nourishment, pleasure in the ingestion. Eaten with plenty of one's own bread, a glass or two of one's own wine—what else does a frittata require to make us feel that we have dined well? Did I hear someone say, "Sir, all that such a dinner needs is a savory, light soup, one that will stimulate the appetite and provide a fluid foundation for all that bread you urge us to eat"?

Right on, Sir! How about *stracciatella?* Never heard of it? Well! That hole in your gastronomy is about to be filled. For a dainty, tantalizing portion for six people, bring to a boil a quart and a half of chicken broth, stir therein two eggs beaten with half a cup of grated Parmesan cheese and immediately turn off the burner. Cover the kettle and serve as soon as the boiling subsides. A sprinkling of finely minced parsley on each serving will please both the eye and the palate.

Tinned chicken broth is available at the supermarket; but it is not half so good as what you can make in your kitchen thus: Cut a stewing hen in three or four pieces. Why an old rather than a young bird? I will give you the answer I heard decades ago, when I was a young boy in Tuscan Italy and occasionally amused myself by eavesdropping on the old peasants who, by their laughter and sly winkings and suggestive gesturing, seemed to be meaning somewhat more than they were saying: *Gallina vecchia fa bon brodo.* An old hen makes a good broth.

As you ponder its hidden meaning, put the pieces of hen in the soup kettle with two quarts of water. When it begins to boil add some salt, a small onion, the leafy upper half of a rib of celery, half a carrot, a bay leaf, half a ripe tomato, and a dozen peppercorns. If you have made *conserva*, as I hope you have, half a teaspoon of that herb-flavored tomato concentrate instead of the ripe tomato will marvelously enhance the flavor of the broth. In about an hour and a half of simmering, the flesh of the old bird will be tender and the broth, somewhat reduced by the simmering, will be done. Pour it through a strainer into a bowl, skim off the fat and use what you need of it for *stracciatella*. The flesh of the old bird, accompanied by various vegetables, may be used for a boiled dinner, chicken salad or, mixed with some ground beef, for a tasty hash.

A broth thus made and frozen in small containers is a staple in every well-ordered kitchen. Have it on hand to be used in making a variety of soups, such as cream of asparagus, stews, sauces, and for the preparation of dishes that require the use of stock. Avoid the tinned variety and always make your own, remembering that *gallina vecchia fa bon brodo.* Italian mothers are in perfect agreement with Jewish mothers: A cup of chicken broth is the infallible cure for all distempers, real or imagined.

I shall now describe the preparation of two dishes, main courses that both require the use of stock. The first recipe is intended to be a stimulus—a point of departure to be varied in whatever way you deem preferable. The other

I shall ask you to follow to the letter on the cocky assumption that what is given cannot be improved upon.

The first is an example of what are generically called stews, *stufati* in Italian. A stew is a food that is cooked by simmering in a flavored liquid or by slow boiling. The word derives from the Middle English *stewen*, which originally meant to bathe in hot water or steam. The Italian *stufato* derives from *stufa*, a stove (also called *fornello*, when the reference is to a stove used for cooking rather than heating). The dictionary definition of *stufato* is "meat cut in small pieces and cooked *in umido*"—humid—some sort of liquid, usually on top of the stove.

A well-made stew provides a dinner that, measured by whatever culinary criteria, stands second to none. The Italian chef or housewife uses the endearing diminutive, *stufatino*, to express its excellence. And yet it is so regrettably undervalued that one is not likely to find it listed on the menu of America's best restaurants. Since you are now committed to cooking your own and to making your kitchen a laboratory of the culinary art, you will add stews to your repertory of dinner menus.

Here is a basic recipe for lamb stew. For six people, cut into small pieces two pounds of boned shoulder. Remove and discard what fat can be easily extracted and brown the pieces of meat in equal parts of olive oil and butter. Remove them with a slotted spoon. Using no more fat than remains in the skillet in which the meat was braised, sauté therein the following, not too finely minced: four green onions, three cloves of garlic, half a carrot, a rib of celery including the leaves, a few sprigs of parsley, enough rosemary leaves to make a tablespoon when coarsely chopped, and a dozen capers. Do this over moderate heat to avoid scorching. When this is done, sprinkle over the whole a scant teaspoon of arrowroot and mix thoroughly with a spatula. This will thicken the emerging sauce. Stir into a cup and a half of stock the juice of half a lemon, a pinch of curry, and a dash of Tabasco. Add this to the above, increase the heat, and turn it off when the sauce begins to bubble.

Put the meat pieces in an appropriate stewing container, add a cup of dry vermouth and stir over high heat until the liquid is somewhat reduced. Now add the flavoring sauce, salt and pepper to taste, and cook, covered, over moderate heat until the meat is tender, about half an hour. Do not overcook. As a final touch you may want to stir in a bit of cream. To make a veal stew, substitute sage leaves for the rosemary and eliminate the curry; and for a beef stew, which will require an hour over moderate heat, eliminate capers, lemon, the two herbs just named and use a cup of sliced mushrooms and red wine instead of vermouth. And now that you know the basics, vary what I have given you as you wish. If you serve the stew I have described to anyone who is sensitive to the taste of food, you will be applauded.

In concluding this culinary discourse, I must ask you to arrest what prejudice you may have against the interior organs of an animal, and serve a dish of the white lining of the stomach of cattle and other ruminants. Unfortunately, its name, tripe, has unsavory connotations in this country. The Italian name, *trippa,* and the French, *tripes,* do not. In both countries, but especially in France, where its preparation has been more or less perfected as *tripes à la mode de*

Caen, it ranks high among people who mind their bellies very carefully and very studiously. I have myself perfected a way of preparing it; and among the friends whom we frequently entertain at dinner, there are several who have become "tripe buffs." To prepare tripe for the oven, where its cooking in a heavy aluminum or cast-iron pot requires about four hours, will take about thirty minutes. This is the way to do it:

Take about four pounds of honeycomb tripe and drop it in a kettle of boiling water acidulated with a cup of cider vinegar. The boiling, of course, will cease. When it resumes, let it continue for a few minutes, then plunge the tripe in cold water until it cools. Remove from it the lumps of fat and cut the tripe into strips about a quarter of an inch wide and put them into the heavy aluminum or cast-iron pot mentioned above. Pour over it a glass of white wine or vermouth and let it boil, uncovered, until most of the wine is evaporated.

Now prepare the flavoring compound in which the tripe will be baked. Dice a piece of salt pork the size of a quarter-pound stick of butter, about a third of it lean. Sauté slowly in a saucepan and discard the fat. Add olive oil and melted butter, two tablespoons of each. Mince and sauté therein half a large onion, a rib of celery, and a small carrot. When these are transparent, add a mince of parsley and thyme, a heaping tablespoon of each, an equal amount of chopped capers, and four cloves of minced garlic. Mix these ingredients thoroughly and continue cooking over low heat to avoid scorching. Sprinkle over the whole a teaspoon of arrowroot for thickening and mix with a spatula. In two cups of stock stir two tablespoons of your aromatized tomato sauce and a dash of Tabasco. Add this to the above ingredients and simmer for a few minutes. The result should be a thickish but fluid sauce. If too thick add more stock. Pour over the tripe, mix thoroughly, clamp on a tight lid and put the pot in an oven preheated to three hundred fifty degrees. While it is cooking examine it from time to time and add stock as needed to keep the compound fluid. It must bake about four hours. At the end of that time, taste it for tenderness and add salt and pepper as required. If tender enough—there is no danger of over-cooking tripe—add a jigger of Calvados—the apple brandy of Normandy—and half a cup of grated Parmesan and an equal amount of bread crumbs. If these absorb too much of the liquid, add more stock, for the final strips of tripe should be well sauced. After these additions, reduce the heat and let the cattle belly ponder its fate before it is given to the belly of *Homo sapiens.*

I once had the pleasure of serving tripe à la Pellegrini to a governor of our state. He loved it. What better testimonial do you need for the excellence of the food and the quality of the state's chief executive?

FOUR

The Cellar

The Grape

AMERICA is "into" wine with a vengeance, determined, it would seem, to expiate the sin of prohibition, reduce its intake of hard liquor, and atone for its long neglect of the holy blood of the grape as the appropriate dinner beverage. There is no need to elaborate on the obvious. Everyone in his middle years will remember that twenty years ago there was no wine in the supermarkets, whereas now they are competing for primacy in the quality and quantity of their wine inventories. Wine tastings, wine and cheese parties, sipping chilled white wine or sherry instead of spirits before dinner, seem to be well on the way to becoming as traditional in America as the high tea in England. There are enological societies and associations of amateur wine-makers. In several states where wine grapes were not grown twenty-five years ago, viticulture is being explored as a principal industry.

It is therefore in the mainstream of this salutary progression in the art of living that the cellar is being included with the fair garden as a gracious addition to one's mansion. And it is to those who are, or ought to be, seriously thinking of making their own wine, that I offer this information. With the addition of the harvest from the states now assaying their land for viticulture, there will one day be an abundance of grapes at vintage time in every state, whether grown there or imported from elsewhere, for the increasing number of householders who, challenged by the high cost of living, are exploring the possibilities of self-reliance in the cellar as well as in the garden and the kitchen. And this move forward in a well-ordered life has a threefold virtue: aesthetic, because the end sought is an increase of pleasure in living; ethical, for the salutary consequences of self-reliance; and practical, for its promotion of household economy.

A lady once asked me for my recipe for wine. My answer was that there is no "recipe" for wine. Crush a ton of grapes into an appropriate container, I told her, and depend on Nature to do the rest. There is, of course, somewhat more to it than that; but that will do as an introduction to the subject of how wine is made. And the first imperative urged upon one who aspires to make it is: Begin with the necessary knowledge of the raw material, the grape. For in a fundamental sense, the quality of a wine is determined in the vineyard. More on this later.

The word "wine," used without a preceding modifier, always refers to the fermented juice of the grape. However, there are other wine-type beverages made by fermenting fruit other than grapes or made from certain vegetables, such as dandelions and rhubarb. When the reference is to one of these, the word "wine" is invariably preceded by the name of the fruit or vegetable fermented to produce it: pear wine, blackberry wine, rhubarb wine. And it is necessary to bear this distinction in mind, for the making of wine differs substantially from the making of wine-type beverages. The latter are made according to what may be properly called a recipe: so much fruit, so much sugar, so much water, and so on. And these I omit from my discussion without prejudice.

I return, then, to a consideration of what the amateur winemaker must know about the grape, for the kind and quality of the grape that he ferments will determine the degree of his success in producing a fine wine. This conclusion has been empirically established for centuries.

Grapevines are members of the botanical family known as *vitaceae*. There are several genera in the group; and the genus that bears grapes is *Vitis*. There are hundreds of species of *Vitis* that thrive in the entire temperate and subtropical zones. We shall consider only the two most important and currently available to the amateur winemaker: the species native to Europe but grown also in several of our states, *Vitis vinifera*, the best wine grape; and *Vitis labrusca*, which is native to America and grown in several states, but most extensively in the east and New England. There are other species of the American grape, such as *V. riparia*, *V. rupestris*, and *V. rotundifolia*. Used mostly for breeding and rootstock, they are not especially noted for the quality of their fruit.

As there are numerous species of the genera, there are also hundreds of varieties of the several species. The wines of Europe, California, and the best grown in certain other states, such as Washington and Oregon, are pressed from vinifera grapes. The best and currently most available varieties of vinifera for the making of fine red wines are Cabernet Sauvignon and Pinot Noir. These are the celebrated wines of Bordeaux and Burgundy. In America they are given the name of the grape. To these I would add Zinfandel, a grape of unknown origin and grown only in America, for I know, from many years of experience in my cellar, that in certain great vintage years the Zinfandel yields a wine worthy of the connoisseur's highest praise.

Lesser but very good red wines may be pressed from Gamay, Merlot, Petite Sirah, Ruby Cabernet, Red Pinot. Somewhat less distinguished than these but worthy of anyone's cellar are generic reds pressed from a blend of such varieties as Mission, Alicante, and Carignane, especially when the blend includes a certain percentage of the more precious varieties. Such blends, labeled by some wineries as Claret or Burgundy or, simply, Red Table wine, are the best of ordinary or jug wines.

The fine white wines are pressed from such vinifera varieties as Chardonnay, Johannisberg Riesling, Grey Riesling, Traminer, Semillon. Excellent but somewhat less than these are Folle Blanche, Sylvaner, Green Hungarian, French Colombard, Chenin Blanc, Sauvignon Blanc, White Pinot, and others. The greatest of the whites is the Chardonnay, the white Burgundy of France.

There are, of course, hundreds of vinifera varieties; and the amateur winemaker will become acquainted with them as they appear on the market and he enlarges his knowledge of the grape and the making of wine. I have listed only the best and currently available. If my preferences seem arbitrary, I can only say that they reflect half a century of experience as an amateur enologist—enology being the art and science of winemaking. Needless to say, the personal experience of so many years has been continuously informed by that of professional enologists in Europe and America. Years ago my mentor was the late Louis Martini, the dean of California winegrowers; more recently I have learned much from Robert Mondavi, currently the most imaginative and innovative in the California wine country.

I remember that when I was a boy in Italy, working both in vineyard and cellar—and very likely something between a hindrance and a help to my father—the elders used to say *ogni uva fa vino*, wine may be pressed from any kind of grape. As I learned later, the dictum, like so many pertaining to Italian viticulture, had both a literal and a metaphorical meaning. The consequence of the literal meaning was that the vineyard of all but the most sophisticated peasant was a hodgepodge of undistinguished varieties, and the wine pressed from them an equally undistinguished blend. If by chance the various vines constituted a harmonious whole, the wine was exceptionally good; and the peasant was considered a genius in the cellar—a partial truth at best.

While it is true that any kind of ripe grapes will yield at least an indifferent wine, the established fact is that good and great wines are made only with the vinifera varieties that I have noted. In the wine industry of America they are known, collectively, as varietals. The name serves to distinguish them from the lesser varieties and to indicate their superior quality as wine grapes. As a class, the varietal vines bear a light crop. For example, a vineyard of Cabernet seldom produces more than four tons to the acre, whereas an acre of many common varieties of vinifera will yield double that amount. Furthermore, the vines of varietals thrive only in certain *limited* areas of the California wine country. Hence the relative scarcity of such grapes on the market and the high, not to say prohibitive, cost of varietal wines. However, as more land congenial to their culture becomes available and more vineyards are established—not only in California, but especially in Oregon and Washington, where thousands of acres are being tested for cultivation of varietals—the supply will necessarily increase. As of now, the few amateur winemakers in Oregon and Washington have no difficulty procuring the necessary grapes. And people who have the means and who look forward to becoming gentlemen farmers are investing in vineyards and giving them attractive names, such as Sagemoor Orchards. The future is heavy with promise for viticulture. And every day in America, Bacchus initiates a new member into the fraternity of wine lovers.

So much for the vinifera varieties. Some of the better-known and currently available varieties of the American *Vitis labrusca*, grown in several states but extensively in the East and New England, are Norton, Clinton, Ives, Isabella, and, most familiar of all, the Concord. These are the reds. For the making of white wines, generally better than the reds, some of the superior varieties are Golden Muscat, Seneca, Delaware, Catawba, Missouri Riesling, Elvira, and Diamond. There are also a number of vines called French Hybrids, vinifera crossed with labrusca and other American species. As these are perfected and their fruit brought to market, the amateur winemaker will be well advised to experiment with them.

The wines pressed from these grapes, with the exception of certain whites produced in the East, are distinctive but never distinguished. Such is the verdict of traditional wine drinkers in the European tradition. This fact, however, does not necessarily dispose of them. The new generation of wine drinkers may find them quite acceptable, for, as we all know, *de gustibus non est disputandum.* Differences in taste are not settled by argument.

Our native grapes, the most familiar being Concord, have been defined as "fox grapes"; and the taste and odor of the juice and wine pressed from them have been described as "foxy." I have found no persuasive explanation for that description. Nor do I agree that the flavor and aroma are, as invariably alleged, unpleasant. Who first levelled that charge? I do not know. It has been said that someone with an acutely discriminating sense of smell detected in the aroma a decisive animal-den effluence. If so, why from the den of a fox, rather than from that of a wolf or a bear? There is no merit in pursuing the matter further. Let me simply suggest that you find the den of a fox, smell it and its resident, and then proceed to judgment. And there I shall let the matter rest.

The American grapes are generally low in sugar, even when fully ripe, and high in acidity. However, when corrected for the deficiency of the one and excess of the other, the fermented juice will yield a pleasant enough wine for anyone who does not find its foxiness unpleasant. In general, the acidity of grapes, their tartness and astringency on the palate, decreases as the sugar content increases. That is the natural consequence of the ripening process. Where this is not achieved in the vineyard, as in the labrusca grapes, the acidity may be decreased by the addition of water to the juice—enough so that it tastes just right on the palate—and the addition of sugar. However, since water necessarily dilutes the flavor of the juice, I do not recommend its use. Better to depend on the addition of sugar, as one does in making lemonade, to do the trick. I shall deal later with the appropriate amounts of sugar and total acidity in the juice in making fine wine. What I have stated here on the matter seemed to me necessary in rounding out my account of labrusca grapes.

From this résumé of grape varieties and viticulture, we may draw certain conclusions which the amateur wine-maker is urged to bear in mind: The quality of a given wine is inherent in the grape used to make it; the world of fine and great wines, in America as elsewhere, is dominated by vinifera grapes; the American species and their several varieties produce, at best, a good but never a great wine; viticulture in America, an infant but growing industry, is now in an advanced experimental stage, the end in view being to find the areas where the combination of soil and climate is most congenial to the growth of each variety of vinifera grapes. The search for such areas is of utmost importance, for the discovery that vinifera grapes, such as Cabernet, flourish throughout an area such as the Napa Valley is but the beginning of the discovery. What remains to be found is the acres in that valley where a given variety achieves its highest potential. And here we encounter one of the imponderables of viticulture and winegrowing. In the Burgundy region of France, where the Pinot Noir vine flourishes, there is a vineyard of about twenty acres that produces Romanée-Conti, the finest Burgundy grown anywhere in the world. And yet, the Pinot Noir grown on acres very close to that precious section of real estate, bathed by the same water and warmed by the same sun, does not yield wine of comparable quality. What is present in the one area that is absent in the other? So far as I know, the question remains unanswered.

Every astute winegrower in California knows that certain vineyards in Napa Valley produce certain varietals that yield the finest wine. Beyond the fact, important but not definitive, that such vineyards may be better tended than others, he does not know why this should be so. The late Louis Martini, who had several Pinot Noir vineyards in the Valley, once told me that his best was near the city of Napa. From that vineyard, which was then producing its first crop, he expected, in time, the finest Pinot Noir wine. Again, why so? I myself once made a Cabernet grown on land near St. Helena. It was a big, rich wine, easily distinguishable from Cabernets made from grapes grown elsewhere in the Valley. In 1964 I had grapes from the Christian Brothers' Mont La Salle Vineyard. Two years later I got them from a vineyard in the Santa Clara Valley. What is left of the Cabernet made from the two lots, now eighteen and sixteen years old respectively, is the best currently in our cellar. They have the attributes of great wines: richness, balance, softness on the palate, complex bouquet. Equal in quality, in the sense that one would hesitate to place the one above the other, they are so different that no experienced wine drinker would fail to tell them apart and to distinguish them from our 1971 and 1973 vintages, which promise to be equally great in a few more years. These differences and discriminations, perceived by the experienced wine drinker, are facts of nature, some of the fascinating imponderables of wines of character and merit; they are never the attributes of what is known in the trade as generic or ordinary wine. Pedigree and breeding are rare virtues in the whole of Nature.

I have given the relevant data on these wines to document the empirically established generalization that the quality of a given wine, and the differences that distinguish it from wines of the same variety, derive from the grape used in making it and the area in which the vines were grown—from the total environment, with all the imponderables that are not subject to measurement.

In any given area, the viticulturist is at the mercy of the weather: in the spring when the vines bloom and the fruit sets, in the summer when the grapes ripen, and in the early fall when they come to full maturity. Unless the balance of cold and heat is just right during each phase of the growing cycle, the harvest will be defective—a bad vintage year. Unseasonably cold or hot weather are equally destructive; and there are no remedial measures against those misfortunes.

In general, vinifera grapes thrive in the cooler regions of the sunny California wine country. And this means areas where the indispensable sun is moderated by atmospheric conditions that protect the grape from the sun's potentially lethal sting. For this reason, vinifera grapes do better in the sunny but relatively cool north coast counties of California, where the ocean breezes temper the heat of the sun, than in the hot Central Valley. But even in the coastal areas, the sun in full summer may be, on occasion, of such intensity that it burns and withers the partially ripe fruit. When that happens, the crop is defective; and if the sun is merciless throughout the entire wine country, the consequence is, again, a bad vintage year.

Given the grape variety and appropriate husbandry in the vineyard, the effect of the weather, good or bad, is lodged in the grape berry. Varietal vines as a class have relatively small bunches and berries—smaller than such table grapes as the Tokay. The individual berry consists of skin, pulp, and seeds. A complete analysis of these constituents is not necessary; but there are certain things about them that the amateur winemaker ought to know. The seeds contain a bitterish substance that will be imparted to the wine if the seeds are broken when the grapes are crushed, so this, of course, must be avoided. If one uses a manual crusher the danger is automatically avoided, for the rollers are so set that the seeds are not broken. Or one may crush the grapes in a large plastic or wooden tub by stomping with the bare feet, a procedure that has been used by the peasants in Europe for centuries. There are also mechanical crushers used by people who make wine in large quantities. The amateur ought to know also that grapes should not be washed, for there is a powdery bloom on the skin of the berry which contains the spores of yeast necessary in fermentation.

The pulp consists of juice, seeds, and certain substances that contribute to the wine's character. The juice of red vinifera grapes is colorless. However, a limited few have some coloring matter in the pulp. Among these, the Alicante has the most; and that grape, which by itself yields only an indifferent wine, is generally used in small quantities for blending with varieties that lack sufficient coloring matter. For example, a considerate grower who sells one a ton of Zinfandel will include a hundred pounds or so of Alicante as "color insurance." However, the great varietals such as Pinot Noir and Cabernet, when fully ripe, invariably have sufficient coloring matter. And this is lodged in the inner layers of the skin. Partially released when the grapes are crushed, it becomes entirely soluble in the juice during fermentation; and from this the finished wine takes its characteristic color.

Coloring matter in grapes used in making white wine is negligible. However, there is enough in the pulp and in the skin to give the finished wine various hues and tints of green and yellow. In other words, white wines are never entirely colorless.

This much, then, the amateur winemaker ought to know about the grape. Lacking this knowledge, he will be working with raw material he does not understand. As in all else, experience is the great teacher. I have known old and wise peasants, illiterate and totally innocent of book knowledge, who would pluck a bunch of grapes, take from it a mouthful of berries, chew them reflectively, squeeze a handful of them, hold the hand closed tightly for a few seconds, open it slowly, noting the degree of resistance effected by the sticky sugar, and, on this purely sensory acquaintance with the grape, predict the quality of the wine. And not in so many words, but with a simple nod of the head, affirmative or negative. Peasants are notoriously taciturn. The peasant would know as much as and probably more than the ordinary enologist whose knowledge of the grape is derived wholly from an analysis of it in the laboratory. Let the amateur winemaker keep this in mind, and look forward to becoming a wise old peasant.

The unfermented juice of the grape is known in the industry as the "must," from the Latin *mustum* and the Italian *mosto*. Let us now suppose that at vintage time we have crushed a quantity of Cabernet grapes, grown in a region where the soil and climate were as required, and the vineyard work—pruning, spraying, fertilizing—was properly done. The grapes were harvested when fully ripe and brought to market. If the amount of sugar and total acidity in the must is just right, we have what is necessary to make a superior wine. What do we mean by "just right"?

It has been established by years of experience that, given the above conditions, the sugar and acidity in the must will be adequate if the range is between 20 and 24 percent by volume of the one and .6 and 1 percent of the other. These are the minimum and the optimum. Where the percentage falls between the two will determine the degree of excellence in the wine. The closer to the optimum, the better the wine. I have found that when the sugar percentage is 23-plus and the total acidity near .8, the result will be a wine that will elicit the highest praise. Of such a wine we would say that the total acidity and the sugar in the must were in nearly perfect balance.

These two constituents of the must are important and measurable. Other elements in it and in the crushed grape are also important but cannot be measured. Let us simply say that they are the necessary imponderables that impart to the wine its total character. I say imponderable because they are as little understood and no more definable than the elements that give a fully ripe peach or strawberry their fragrance and taste. Either they are present in the grape or they are not.

The required sugar and acidity are important for several reasons. A fine wine must have from 12 to 14 percent by volume of alcohol in order that it may have stability, durability, and viscosity (viscosity being the oily quality that contributes so much to the wine's softness and richness). The acidity is further necessary to give the finished wine its required astringency. Adequate sugar, or too much, combined with low acidity, will yield a wine that is flat and lacks bite and assertiveness on the palate, as do certain ripe fruits that are sweet but lacking in tartness. This is true of wines made with grapes grown in the hot Central Valley of California, for they are generally high in sugar and deficient in acidity. And, of course, grapes that are low in sugar and high in acidity, either because they are inherently so, such as the varieties of labrusca, or were picked when not fully ripe, will yield a wine that is unpleasantly astringent.

So dinner wines must have from 12 to 14 percent alcohol by volume. How is that achieved? During the fermentation, the amount of sugar in the must yields, in roughly equal parts, carbon dioxide gas and alcohol. The gas, of course, escapes in the process. Thus, if in a given must the sugar is about 23 percent, the finished wine will contain somewhat more than 13 percent alcohol; and if we assume that the acidity is adequate, the finished product will be a relatively rich wine, remembering that the richness of a wine, its fattiness, and its viscosity are all functions of its alcoholic content. And, indeed, when the alcohol ranges from 13 to 14 percent by volume, the wine is invariably and variously described as being big, rich, robust, and, begging a liberated lady's pardon, masculine. On words

and phrases used by connoisseurs, and others self-appointed as such, to describe wine, I shall have more to say later.

Grapes Into Wine: Some Preliminary Considerations

Autumn: "Season of mists and mellow fruitfulness."
How cheerfully the poet put it! In the Old Country, the
untutored peasant said it all and as cheerfully in a mouth-
watering aphorism: *A Settembre l'uva è matura e il fico
pende.* Come September, the grapes are ripe and the fig
droops on the bough. Be it known here that the fig issues,
tiny but fully formed, directly from the limb at an oblique,
upward angle; and when it is fully grown and ripe, the
stem loses its erectile energy, begins to wither, and the fig
hangs downward at whatever angle is determined by the
posture of the limb. The riper the fruit, the more pronounced its droop and the more likely there will be a drop
of honey at its base. Hence the cheerful aphorism and the
delight of the peasant, for he may now enrich his meager
diet with figs and his cellar with the next year's supply of
wine.

The amateur winemaker in America, relatively well fed
and well housed, needs not the season of mists and mellow
fruitfulness to enrich his diet, for he is more likely to suffer
from too much than from too little food. However, once
he has brought to the table a good wine of his own making,
he will look forward to each fall with a fresh excitement.
He will share the anxiety of the viticulturist throughout the
growing cycle, for he now knows that the quality of the
grapes he expects to crush will be determined by the
weather during that time in the area where the vineyard is

located. I speak from experience. Knowing precisely where the vineyard whence my grapes come is located in the Napa Valley, I check the weather in that area during the critical periods in the growing cycle. Three years ago a heavy rain fell during the week when the grapes, because the sugar and acidity were in perfect balance, had to be harvested. Those that were dispatched immediately to the winery were not adversely affected; but mine, packed wet in thirty-pound lugs and shipped by truck, developed considerable mold in transit. One despairing look at them when they arrived, and I knew immediately that there was no possibility of converting them into great wine. My problem was: How shall I deal with the mold? Shall I discard the moldy bunches? Or shall I crush the whole and attempt a salvage operation? Having been told by the vineyard superintendent that the sugar was ample and the acidity adequate, I chose the latter course. More on this matter later.

For the last two vintage seasons, the grapes sent to me, the weather having been ideal throughout the growing cycle, were in every respect in perfect condition: sugar and acidity as required and every bunch sound. One glance at them and, after testing them in the manner of "a wise old peasant," I knew that I could expect them to yield a superior and, possibly, a great wine. Incidentally, sound, fully ripe grapes, properly packed in twenty-five- or thirty-pound lugs, may be shipped long distances and arrive in good condition—or even a bit improved for the slight dehydration and consequent concentration of sugar they may undergo in transit. I have ascertained this by carrying lugs of grapes a thousand miles in the trunk of my car and keeping them in our cellar for a week. Furthermore, growers in California have been shipping wine grapes in cattle cars to the home winemaker as far away as the east coast. If the grapes are sound and properly packed, they invariably arrive at their destination in good condition. Otherwise, and inevitably, they arrive in bad shape. Years ago, during and immediately after prohibition, there was a railroad siding in south Seattle where grape brokers sold grapes directly from the freight car. When I bought from them, I dealt with the one who offered the best. On occasion, when I had no clear choice, I had to accept and do what I could with what was available.

I have noted these facts for several reasons. As the amateur winemaker progresses in his cellar work, he will increasingly share the anxiety of the grower about the weather during the entire growing cycle. A bit of the considerable mythology of wine and winegrowing, urged by the public-relations firm of this or that winery, goes something like this: "The grapes for our wines are picked instantly at full maturity and rushed to the winery where they are immediately crushed and fermented." While such dispatch may be desirable, it is infrequently possible. The exigencies of the vintage season may, and frequently do, prevent it: the necessary hands not there to pick the grapes instantly; transportation to the winery not immediately available; the winery not able to process the grapes the instant they are delivered. Nor is all this urgency necessary unless various crises require it. If the grapes be fully ripe and sound, and the weather fair, a day or so delay in all these procedures does no harm whatever. I have often seen truckloads of grapes on standby at the winery, with bees and other winged creatures feasting on them, waiting to be wheeled to the crusher. (Noting the grip of the bees on the berries, I wondered how many of the bees would be crushed and fermented along with the grapes. Would enough of them go to their honeyed death to impart to the finished wine what a discerning connoisseur would describe as an "effluence of beehive"?) Nor was I aware that the enologist in charge in any way regretted the delay and the pilfering bees. And rightly so, for he knew that, the grapes being ripe and in good condition, all would be well in the cellar.

Another reason for all this information is that the amateur winemaker who lives, as I do, a long distance from the vineyard, there being no grape broker in the vicinity, will have to cope with the problem of getting the grapes to his cellar. The grower is not always equipped to pack the grapes properly; and transportation systems cannot be relied on to handle the grapes with care and deliver them promptly. Once, for example, grapes were sent to me from California inexcusably packed in heavy plastic bags. Delayed and miserably crushed in transit, they were a revolting mess when delivered. What to do? Too bad! And better luck next time. Therefore, in order to avoid uncertainty, frustration, and possible disaster, the home winemaker is well advised to procure a pickup truck and go directly to the vineyard for his grapes—when possible.

Thus far I have given an account of what one who has decided to make his own wine and add a most pleasant and exciting dimension to his life, must know about the grape. Based on many years of experience with grapes and grapes into wine, enriched by what I have learned from experts in vineyard and cellar, the information here recorded is authentic and entirely reliable. I therefore urge, disinterestedly, the amateur winemaker to accept it as the indispensable minimum he ought to have in order to become an informed practitioner of the craft.

Let us now suppose that we are in the season of mists and mellow fruitfulness. There are twelve hundred pounds of red vinifera grapes in the cellar. The sugar and acidity are what they ought to be. We can now go through the entire process of converting them into the finished wine. But first, some preliminary matters. As to the grapes: The grower always picks the grapes when the sugar and acidity are adequate; and he passes the information on to the purchaser. So there is no need to test them. In any case, in any given year, the grapes are what they are and one hopes for the best. Wondering how near perfect they may be is a part of the excitement that adds zest to the vintage season.

Wine cannot be made in the kitchen, nor aged and stored in a closet when made. You will need a cellar in an enclosed corner of the basement where the temperature is never much above or below sixty degrees Fahrenheit. Lacking such a cellar, an unheated and insulated garage will do. What you must bear in mind is that the temperature must remain more or less constant at that level. If one has the means to conrol the temperature in whatever area the wine is made, so much the better.

The equipment needed will depend, in part, on the amount of wine that is to be made each vintage season. What I recommend is no less than sixty gallons, roughly a bottle a day for the ensuing year. I urge that much for two reasons. First, there is no risk of failure in making wine;

hence, no reason to be cautious about the amount you make even in your initial effort. If the grapes are just right, and the cellar work is done as I shall explain, success will be assured. Furthermore, the freshly made wine must be aged at least a year in an oak barrel, for reasons to be noted later. And while the cooper makes barrels of various capacities, the ones most practical for the home winemaker are the ones that have a capacity of thirty, fifty, or sixty gallons.

Thus, if we agree on this sixty-gallon minimum, you must crush about twelve hundred pounds of grapes. The yield in finished wine will be somewhat more than sixty gallons, enough to fill the one large or the two smaller barrels. In other words, one must make enough wine to justify the acquisition of the absolutely indispensable oak barrels —known collectively in the industry as "cooperage." In addition to these, the novitiate will need the following equipment: a manual crusher, a container for fermentation, and a wine press. All of these are available in various sizes. The crusher, a hopper with two parallel rollers at the base, ought to be large enough to hold about twenty-five pounds of grapes, and the press of a size to hold twice that amount of crushed grapes. I urge you to visit a winemaker's supply shop to become acquainted with these tools of the craft and learn how they are used.

For the fermentation, there is a choice of containers. The most satisfactory is a single tank of stainless steel or such nonresinous wood as oak, maple, or redwood. Containers made of ferrous material must be avoided, for the interaction of iron and the acids in the must and the wine affects the wine adversely. If a satisfactory tank is not available, the winemaker can use discarded whiskey barrels, generally available at nurseries and some supermarkets. These have a capacity of about fifty gallons; and for twelve hundred pounds of grapes you would need three. I have four in my cellar that have been in use for fifty years. Also available and satisfactory are heavy-duty plastic containers of about thirty-gallon capacity. And of these one would need four or five for the twelve hundred pounds of grapes crushed. Whatever container is used, remember to fill it to no more than within a foot of the top. That much space is necessary to accommodate the upward thrust of the mass caused by the carbon dioxide gas during the most vigorous phase of fermentation, and to prevent an embarrassing overflow.

The above constitute the major, permanent, and heritable part of the equipment. If well made and of durable material, they can be used for many generations. My crusher and press were made of hard wood about a century ago, the one by a German cabinet-maker in Portland, the other by an Italian craftsman in Seattle. Assuming, as Gertrude said to Hamlet—and is it not a fair assumption?—that all that lives must die, passing through nature to eternity, we too will go the way of all flesh, leaving to our children nothing more durable and precious than the crusher and the press. And to indicate their relevance, we may include a case or two of wine.

Other indispensables in the equipment are: ten or more five-gallon glass containers called carboys; several gallon jugs with appropriate closures; a couple hundred standard wine bottles and corks; two six-foot lengths of rubber hose, one a quarter-inch, the other a half-inch in diameter;

a large plastic funnel for pouring wine into carboys and jugs; a smaller one for pouring it into bottles; and a corking device. All of these except the corks, if used with care, will last indefinitely. So while the initial outlay is substantial, it occurs only once. Furthermore, note the end results. You have fermented twelve hundred pounds of, let us say, Cabernet. The yield is sixty gallons, or three hundred bottles. The current price of the most ordinary Cabernet wine is no less than five dollars a bottle—*relatively* inexpensive because it is not 100 percent Cabernet. There is no deception here by the winery, for the law permits labeling a given wine as a varietal if the grapes included 51 percent or more of that variety. A vintage bottle of 100 percent Cabernet, such as yours, sells for upwards of ten dollars. Need I spell out the dollar value of what you have made? And need I add to that what cannot be measured in dollars and cents: the profound satisfaction in the achievement?

Grapes Into Wine: The Cellar Work

Now that we have the necessary knowledge of the grape, and the cellar is appropriately equipped, we may proceed with the cellar work in full confidence and in a very special species of exuberance, for the vintage season, when all goes well, is inherently gay. Dipping into the cornucopia of Nature, we participate in her vast and varied creativity by converting one of her precious gifts into what Steinbeck, in a moment of vinous inspiration, called the Holy Blood of the grape. Thus, in our cellar work, we are genuine creators; for to create is to bring something into being—a poem; a painting; a crackling, nut-brown loaf; a bottle of fine wine. The ones energize the spirit; the others, the body. And who is to say which order of creation is the more relevant to well-being, to a well-ordered life? It is wise to perceive the two orders in perspective, as they relate to living appropriately, in harmony with Nature, for the ivory-tower elitist is too prone to exalt the one and neglect the other. The mother who bears children, gives them her breast, guides them wisely toward physiological maturity, maintains a happy ambience in the home; the peasant whose land husbandry is impeccable; the mason who places brick on brick with generations yet unborn in mind: these, and their kind, though they may lack formal learning, have their proper place in the hierarchy of genuine creators. From each according to his highest potential; and what matters is not the kind nor the magnitude of the thing created, but its authenticity and relevance to a well-ordered life.

I insist on this in order that we may approach our labor, in the cellar as elsewhere, with joy in our hearts and an appropriately ethical orientation. The more so in the project at hand; for wine, served at the Last Supper, used in certain religious rites, offered in salute to friends at the dinner table and to enhance the dinner's gaiety, has become the symbol of hospitality. "Good friends, go in, and taste some wine with me," said Caesar to Brutus and his co-conspirators, not knowing that they were about to murder him. And a later poet—Keats—in a moment of high exuberance:

> O for a beaker full of the warm South,
> Full of the true, the blushful Hippocrene,
> With beaded bubbles winking at the brim,
> And purple-stained mouth.

And my bibulous grandmother, pouring a guest a glass of wine and smiling mischievously: "Wink at me if you like it." And the corpulent clergyman, reproached by his bishop for being habitually too full of the blushful Hippocrene: "Monsignor, when I consider that wine is the blood of Jesus, there is no end to what I could drink. Will you join me in a confirmatory goblet?" And so it goes with wine, the fermented juice of the grape, its Holy Blood, celebrated by poet and peasant; and, happily in the wine country, on the table of the poor as well as of the rich.

The fermented juice of the grape! That and nothing more! For the wine we are about to make will be the fermented juice of the grape, with nothing added thereto and nothing subtracted therefrom. That is the definition of all superior dinner wines, variously described as vintage or great wine. In latitudes where the harvested grape lacks the sugar and acidity *necessary* to produce a satisfactory wine, the accepted procedure is to make the correction by addition or subtraction. Normally, the deficiency is in sugar. When such corrections are properly made, the result is a good-enough wine; but it is never a vintage or great wine. It is well to bear this in mind on those rare occasions when some sugar may have to be added. Rare, I say, for the reason that wherever vinifera grapes are grown in America, the sugar content, though not necessarily ideal, is normally adequate when the grapes are harvested and sent to market.

We have now in the cellar twelve hundred pounds of red vinifera grapes. The grower has assured us that the sugar and acidity are adequate. We are now ready to convert the grapes into wine ready to be bottled. It has probably been assumed that I am writing only about dinner wine; if so, the assumption is correct. The making of aperitif, dessert, tonic, sparkling, and other wines is too complicated for the home winemaker to venture into until he has had considerable cellar experience. Furthermore, having never made those other wines myself, how could I possibly instruct others?

Crushing the grapes is, of course, the first operation. However, before that is undertaken, all the necessary equipment must be thoroughly clean and set in place. Absolute cleanliness in the cellar is a must. If old barrels are used, they may be sanitized with a cup of soda ash in five gallons of boiling water. Slosh the solution in the barrel for a minute or so and then rinse it several times with cold water. In addition to the equipment for the crushing operation, you must have at hand for the twelve hundred pounds of grapes a cup of dry wine yeast and eleven scant teaspoons of potassium metabisulphite dissolved in half a pint of water. I shall explain the use of these later. Although not strictly necessary, but to give the cellar a semblance of laboratory sophistication, it is well to have on hand a saccharometer for testing the sugar content of the must. All of these materials may be bought at a wine-arts shop. When everything is thus in order, a crew of four with capable hands can crush the twelve hundred pounds of grapes in about three hours.

It is standard practice in commercial wineries to remove the stems from the crushed grapes. This is done by a mechanized crusher-stemmer. The reason urged for removing them is that the stems contain a concentration of tannin and other substances that impart to the wine

"astringency, bitterness, and resinous or peppery flavors."
Notwithstanding the fact that all wineries in California de-
stem the grapes, the reason offered for the practice is not
entirely persuasive. Not all competent winemakers agree
that stems impart objectionable flavors to the wine.
Some insist that the tannin in the stems adds to the necessary tannin in red wine. Robert Mondavi, more experimental and imaginative than most winegrowers, constantly striving to produce the flawless wine, is determined to
settle the matter to his own satisfaction in the only definitive way: He divides a given quantity of grapes into several
parts. One lot he ferments without removing the stems;
from each of the other he removes a different percentage.
And when the wine is made, he and his associate tasters
will judge the results. The procedure requires time and
effort; but it is the only way.

In my own cellar I have made very good wines without
removing the stems. During the past twenty years, having
had access to the finest Cabernet grapes, I have followed a
middle course by removing about half the stems. The
resulting wines, served by my New York publisher to two
European connoisseurs, received the highest praise.
Indeed, the two experts had to be convinced, reluctantly,
that they were made by a school teacher in his basement in
—of all places!—Seattle. I pass this information on to the
amateur winemaker not by way of self-congratulation, but
to persuade him that what I have done, he, too, will be
able to do, for as I have repeatedly emphasized, wine is
made in the vineyard, not the cellar.

I therefore recommend that you begin by removing
about half the stems. Later, when you have had more cel-

lar experience, you may want to experiment in the manner of Robert Mondavi. The crushing and desteming procedure is, of necessity, slow-paced. It is all work with the hands; and while one may work with a certain manual dexterity, one must not sacrifice performance to speed. Furthermore, there are three main operations in converting grapes into wine: harvesting the grapes, crushing the grapes, drawing the wine after the first fermentation. In Italy, the complete wine country, each is indicated by a single word: *vendemmia, pigiatura, svinatura.* There, of course, since he who makes his own wine invariably grows his own grapes, the first two are accomplished simultaneously. The peasant picks the grapes into an elliptical wooden container of manageable size, called a *bigoncia*, and crushes them in that container by repeated thrusts of a wooden plunger shaped like a baseball bat. When half full, more or less, the *bigoncia* is conveyed to the cellar, on the shoulder if the distance is not forbidding, and its contents, all stems included, are dumped, with an audible sigh of relief, into the *tino*, the fermenting vat. I know whereof I speak, for when I visited my native land for the first time, during the season of mists and mellow fruitfulness in 1949, a movie camera recorded my labor in what had been the family vineyard, bearing the *bigoncia* on my shoulder, grunting my laborious way to the cantina.

We, peasants in spirit only, since we have no vineyard, are concerned only with the crushing and the drawing of the wine. And what we must keep at the center of our consciousness is that the two operations are, traditionally, festive affairs, in both the Apollonian and Dionysian mode: Apollo, the God of the Sun, Poetry, Music; and Dionysus, the God of Wine and Nature's marvelously pervasive fertility. Furthermore, in the labor involved we realize what the old Church Fathers meant when they said *Laborare est Orare:* work is worship. Accordingly, let there be full-throttle gaiety energized with bread and cheese and wine, bursts of song, vinous witticisms—the third glass will provide the inspiration—and poetry during the entire operation: O for a beaker full of the warm South! Do you remember the rest? Or as Abraham Cowley put it in the mid-1600s:

> The thirsty earth soaks up the rain
> And drinks and gapes for drink again;
> The plants suck in the earth, and are
> With constant drinking fresh and fair;
> The sea itself (which one would think
> Should have but little need of drink)
> Drinks twice ten thousand rivers up,
> So filled that they o'erflow the cup;
> The busy Sun (and one would guess
> By's drunken fiery face no less)
> Drinks up the sea, and when he's done,
> The Moon and Stars drink up the Sun;
> They drink and dance by their own light,
> They drink and revel all the night:
> Nothing in Nature's sober found,
> But an eternal health goes round.
> Fill up the bowl, then, fill it high,
> Fill all the glasses there—for why
> Should every creature drink but I?
> Why, man of morals, tell me why?

And why not improve a bit on A. E. Housman as we sip a vintage wine:

> A glass of wine filled to the brim,
> Does much more than Milton can
> To justify the ways of God to man.

If, while these Dionysian rites are in progress, some ascetic sourpuss should come along sniffing disapproval, why not ask him, gently but firmly, "Dost thou think, because thou art holy, there shall be no more cakes and wine?"

In some such ways as here suggested, we approach the cellar work in what I have called the Apollonian–Dionysian mode. The fermenting vat is ready in its proper place in the cellar. The crushing of the grapes, being an inevitably messy operation, is better done outside on the patio, which can be hosed when the job is done. If one elects to crush by stomping with the bare feet, a procedure that has the sanction of centuries, one must do it in a flat-bottomed tub; and to make sure that every berry is crushed or bruised, let there be no more than twenty-five or thirty pounds in the tub at a time. If a hand crusher is used, and in order to facilitate the removing of the stems, the following procedure is suggested: Set the crusher athwart two saw horses about three feet high. Place between them, directly under the crusher, a plastic container about twenty inches in diameter and large enough to hold thirty or so pounds of grapes. This will receive them as they drop from the crusher. The reason for the suggested diameter is that hand crushers for the home winemaker are of standard size, the crushing rollers at the bottom being about a foot long. And since the crushed grapes will drop from all along that length, the receiving vessel must be of some such diameter as I have suggested. Furthermore, to avoid spillage occasioned by the squirt and scatter of the falling grapes, it is advisable to elevate the vessel so that it is close to the bottom of the crusher. Attention to these details will assure neatness and orderliness in the operation.

Assuming a crew of four or more, you will need at least two such receiving vessels. Two of the four crew members will man the crusher, the others will remove the stems. As a vessel is filled, it is taken by one of the stem removers and the empty one immediately set in place to catch the inevitable drippings while the crusher is being refilled. To remove the stems, swirl the mass vigorously by hand to bring the stems to the surface. Taking a handful at a time, shake the stems thoroughly so that neither juice nor whatever berries still cling to them are lost. To avoid waste, the pace must be necessarily slow. When about half the stems have been removed, the receiving vessel is emptied into the fermenting vat. The fermenting vat, of course, whether tank or barrel, is stood on end and open at the top.

Such is the crushing and destemming procedure when a hand crusher is used; nor is it significantly different when the winemaker elects to crush with the feet. I must now explain how and why the wine yeast and the metabisulphite are used. The function of both is to assure a clean and sound fermentation. Grapes, carrying on their skins various species of yeast, will ferment without being inoculated with true wine yeast. However, of the several species of yeast, many are "wild" and fewer are benign. These are the true wine yeasts. They belong to a family known as *Saccharomyces.* If the fermentation is controlled by the wild yeasts, the wine may have unpleasant tastes, odors, and possibly turn to vinegar. To avoid this disaster, the must is inoculated with a true wine yeast and potassium metabisulphite. The one aids the saccharomyces, the other inhibits the growth of the wild yeasts. Thus, the metabisulphite may be considered a harmless preservative, and its presence in the wine will not be detected when used in the quantity recommended. When it is first introduced into the crushed grapes, you will smell the sulphur dioxide gas generated. Do not be alarmed, for when the fermentation is completed, there will be no trace of it.

Some commercial wineries, to make sure that their wines do not turn sour, tend to use too much metabisulphite, especially in their white wines. And the experienced wine drinker will detect it in the finished wine. I have habitually used it, at the rate of a hundred parts per million, when the grapes are crushed, and added no more thereafter. And with invariably good results. Once I submitted a sample of the young wine, a month or so old, to a winery for analysis. The enologist assured me that I had done my cellar work well; but he said that if the wine were his, he would add a specified amount of metabisulphite. Needless to say, I did not take his advice, because I knew from experience that the addition was unnecessary. Having always contained no more than the minimum, my wines had been invariably sound.

However, I understood his concern as the responsible enologist in the winery, for he was dealing with thousands of gallons which, when bottled and shipped to various parts of the country, would be beyond his control. Since rare is the wine merchant who has a wine cellar in which the temperature is maintained at the desired level—about sixty degrees Fahrenheit—the wine, stored indifferently in warehouses and on retailers' shelves in varying temperatures, might reach the consumer in bad shape. Given these entirely realistic vicissitudes of the trade, the enologist could not afford to take chances. Hence his insistence on having in the wine enough of what is called in the trade sulphur dioxide, to keep it stable. This, I say, I understood. But I was dealing with no more than a hundred gallons, to be kept in my own cellar, tasted periodically and, when properly aged, brought to the dinner table. Therefore, and never having sustained a failure, I did not have the burden of anxiety that plagued the enologist responsible for those thousands of gallons.

Sulphur has been used in vineyard and cellar for centuries. When I began making wine decades ago, fermenting tanks and all cooperage were treated with sulphur dioxide by burning in them a suspended sulphur wick. Potassium metabisulphite is a relatively recent and more efficient means of achieving the same results. The formula of so many parts per million was devised in the laboratory. Some winemakers use a hundred as the required minimum in the must; others may use a hundred and fifty. On the basis of the lower ratio, a scant teaspoon is enough for five gallons of must. Since twelve hundred pounds of grapes will yield about sixty gallons, and to avoid using too much, I figured that eleven scant teaspoons would provide the effective minimum of metabisulphite. The figures are approximate; but years of consistently satisfactory results in the cellar attest their reliability.

When the crushing operation is begun, we have on hand, as already mentioned, the yeast and the dissolved metabisulphite. As soon as enough grapes have been crushed to yield about two quarts of must, strain it, heat it a bit to remove the chill, pour it into a gallon jug in the kitchen, add the yeast, and set it aside. In a few hours the yeast will be activated. This is the starter, to be added to the must a few hours after the crush is completed. The metabisulphite solution, to assure its complete diffusion throughout the mass, is added in driblets to the must, at more or less even intervals, during the entire operation. When the fermenting vat is filled to within a foot of the top, stir the whole with a convenient length of two-by-four. (Mine, in use for several decades, is almost a vinous edible.) If you use two or more fermenting containers, determine the approximate number of gallons in each, and distribute the yeast solution accordingly—remembering, of course, that the total amount prepared was intended for sixty gallons of must. Thus, if three barrels of fifty-gallon capacity are used, each will hold about a third of the twelve hundred pounds; and to each will be given a third of the prepared solution.

When the crush is completed, clean the work area thoroughly and wash the equipment used. Burn or bury or otherwise dispose of the discarded stems, and gather up whatever spillage could not have been avoided. For the season of mists and mellow fruitfulness is also the season of fruit flies. Crushed ripe fruit, especially grapes, seems miraculously to generate them by the millions over night. Nasty nuisances! If not checked by the removal of the generating matrix, they will turn up in your nostrils, in your ears, in your fruit juice—and they have a fondness for wine. What a nose! Pull the cork from a bottle of wine, and in an instant they appear—from whence?—and drown their sorrow in it. By absolute cleanliness and spreading a sheet over the fermenting vat, I have managed to keep them at bay.

The yeast starter, prepared at the beginning of the crush, should be added three or four hours after the crush is completed. By that time the yeast will be sufficiently activated to go to work on the sugar. Shake the gallon jug and pour all the starter on the must on one spot. Do not stir. Thus concentrated in a small area, the saccharomyces will initiate the fermentation immediately. Stir thoroughly on the following day. (If you are using more than one fermenting barrel, after shaking the gallon jug, pour the starter, in equal portions, into one spot in each of the barrels.)

In my mansion, we traditionally plan the crush so that it will be completed near the dinner hour. Why? So that we may conclude the celebration most appropriately with some such hearty fare as pasta al pesto, Italian sausage with green peppers, and homebaked bread. Now that there are some thirty million Americans of Italian parentage, that increasingly appreciated sausage is available in all but the most provincial sections of the nation. Cut it in small pieces, cook them slowly in a large skillet, transfer them, using a slotted spoon, to a bowl. Discard the dreaded, artery-clogging fat, deglaze the pan with half a glass of white wine, add the savory and less objectionable olive oil —a couple of tablespoons—throw in three or four cloves of garlic coarsely chopped, add one large pepper per person, cut in strips, salt and pepper as desired, turn the heat to high, give the skillet a few vigorous swirls, stir the sausage in with the peppers, put on the lid, reduce the heat. In five minutes the hearty dish will be ready to serve.

The best vintage having been brought up from the cellar, the several bottles, now at room temperature, are on the table. By way of grace, the Master proposes an inter-generational toast.

> *Bevevan i nostri padri,*
> *Bevevan le nostre madri,*
> *E noi che figli siam,*
> *Beviam, beviam, beviam!*

The Italian is easily pronounced: Our fathers and our mothers drank, And we who are their children, Let us drink, let us drink, let us drink! That relates the present to the past—an imperative that must never be forgotten—while the future is being generated in the cellar.

After dinner the Master will go to the cellar to add the yeast starter. The fermentation will begin immediately but imperceptibly. In about four or five days it will be in its most vigorous, tumultuous phase. It can be heard, a seething, sizzling sound like the hum of a million bees; and the aroma borne on the carbon dioxide gas will permeate the premises. Neighbors will sniff approvingly, and others passing by will wonder what's cooking. Thereafter, it will proceed with diminishing vigor but still audibly to one who listens with ear close to the rim of the vat. Depending on the temperature in the cellar area, it will be completed within a week. That means that all but a fraction of the sugar has been converted into alcohol and carbon dioxide gas. As the fermentation subsides, taste the wine from time to time; and when you no longer detect any sugar in it, you will know that the saccharamyces have done their work. Or you may don a white jacket, assume the posture of a laboratory technician, and test the new wine with the saccharometer. In any case, submit it to what the experts call the organoleptic test (what others call a taste test), and thus begin the education of a winemaker's palate, for in practice, if not in theory, that must invariably be the definitive test to which wine is submitted.

Beginning on the day after the starter was added to the crushed grapes, and every day thereafter during the fermentation, the contents of the fermenting vat must be thoroughly stirred in the morning and in the evening. If convenient, do it three times daily. This is required for the following reasons: The bulk of solids in the vat—pulp, skins, seeds, stems—is variously called pomace or the marc. The gas generated by the fermentation pushes the pomace to the top, thus separating it from the emerging wine below and exposing its surface to the air. The exposure, if prolonged, may induce souring; in addition, the separation prevents the fermenting must from extracting those various essences in the pomace that give the finished wine the total character that will appear when it is properly aged. Therefore, the daily stirring of the mass must be done regularly and with vigor. Furthermore, fermentation generates heat in the middle of the vat; and heat induces the growth of undesirable bacteria. Frequent stirring, by bringing to the surface what is below, will effect the necessary cooling.

Professional enologists recommend that, when the fermentation is nearly completed—there still being some residual sugar in the wine—the wine be drawn immediately; what remains of the sugar can be left to ferment slowly in the storage barrel. The reason urged is that the sooner it is separated from the pomace, the better the wine. As in the matter of removing the stems, some winemakers, those who do not go uncritically by the book, do not follow this advice. Especially when the grapes are in all ways perfect, they delay the drawing of the wine for several days after the fermentation is completed. Robert Mondavi, having visited some of the best Bordeaux wineries, is convinced that that is the proper procedure. And so am I. The reason for the delay is simply that the wine needs more time to extract and assimilate the various virtues of the grape. I therefore recommend that the daily stirring be continued and the wine drawn no sooner than the tenth day from the time the grapes were crushed. Some experienced cellarmasters recommend two weeks.

This conforms with the practice of the wise old peasants to whom I learned to listen when I was a boy, and from whom I learned the meaning of careful husbandry and self-reliance in a world where the day's bread was always uncertain, and from whom I learned about living, as Montaigne taught, in harmony with Nature. When, in the vintage season, the eager young suggested that it was time to draw the wine, the eldest and wisest would say, "Not yet! The newborn wine must fatten on the opulent grape." Such is the rationale of winemakers who have learned by experience that the delay in drawing the wine does, indeed, fatten it. Take it or leave it; one learns by doing.

If, however, the crushed grapes were not opulent; if they were bleeding and spotted with mold, then the wine would be drawn as soon as the fermentation began to subside. And for obvious reasons. When the grapes he buys are, for whatever reason, defective, this breed of ill luck must be borne with patience by the home winemaker. I mentioned earlier that a few years ago I received a shipment of grapes that were rich in sugar but spotted with considerable mold. One could smell it in the must, in the fermenting mass and, later, in the young wine. The best I could do with such grapes was in the nature of a salvage operation. The wine was drawn off the pomace as soon as the fermentation began to subside; and it was siphoned in the presence of air from one carboy to another several times during the next few days. The process is called "racking": pumping or siphoning the wine off the sediment that falls to the bottom of the container. More on racking later. Meanwhile, remember the term. When the racking is being done, as in the matter of my moldy grapes, aerate the wine by elevating the one carboy and letting the wine flow through the hose into the one on the floor. The consequent aeration will eliminate or substantially reduce the bad odor. When my wine thus treated had been two years in the barrel, people who drink wine regularly could detect no mold in either the taste or bouquet. There was, in fact, a trace of it; but it was so faint that it detracted little from the wine that was otherwise very good. So the salvage operation had been successful.

On rare occasions—it has happened to me only once in fifty years—the young wine, toward the end of the fermentation, mysteriously develops an odor of rotten eggs: hydrogen sulphide. Should that happen to you, do not despair; it can be eliminated by the racking procedure. I mention these instances of ill luck so that the amateur may know how to deal with them.

The drawing of the wine and pressing of the pomace—the *svinatura*—are a simple but slow-paced procedure. It is also a gay affair. Using a plastic colander, remove the pomace to the wine press and slowly apply the pressure. (Presses are so constructed that a receiving vessel may be placed below the spout to receive the flow of wine.) The flow will be initially gushing, since the pomace is saturated

with wine. As it diminishes and becomes a trickle, apply more pressure. Continue in this manner, giving each turn of the screw enough time to do its work; and when you feel that what wine is reasonably recoverable has been recovered, empty the press and repeat the process. Do not hurry what in the nature of things cannot be hurried. And do not insist on extracting the last drop, for it will have in it bitterish elements undesirable in the wine. Transfer this wine— press wine—from the receiving vessel—a large plastic tub or bucket—into carboys. Plug the carboys temporarily with wads of absorbent cotton. The pressed pomace may be composted for the garden.

The wine left in the fermenting vat is known in the trade as the free-run, in order to distinguish it from the press wine. Strain it and funnel it into the carboys. The strainer must be nonferrous and fine enough to hold back the seeds. I have extemporized an effective one by simply lining my large funnel with a piece of plastic screening material, such as is used in making screen doors. When it becomes clogged, I rinse it in a pan of water.

With all the wine in carboys, the *svinatura* is completed. The equipment must be washed and put away; and since the wine will be kept in carboys for several weeks, these will have to be fitted with closures called fermentation valves. The function of these is to keep the air out and let the gas generated by further fermentation in the carboys escape. This is called the secondary fermentation. There are two types: one is simply the fermentation of whatever residual sugar is in the freshly-drawn wine; the other, called malolactic, is a bacterial fermentation caused by certain strains of bacteria acting on the malic acid in the young wine. This is very gentle, produces some gas but no alcohol, and is normally completed in about two months. To accommodate the secondary fermentation, the fermentation valve of a carboy contains water in a U-shaped glass tube; and the escaping gas may be seen bubbling up through the water. Thus, when bubbles no longer appear, the winemaker will know that the secondary fermentation is completed.

The *svinatura* is in the nature of a harvest, for the end product of the grape has been gathered and put away for future use. A commendable tradition requires a celebration, of which the center of interest is wine and the drinking thereof at the dinner table. Or, according to current usage, the occasion calls for a party, a dinner party on the evening of the day when the work is completed. The participants will be, of course, your entire family and whatever friends assisted in the *svinatura*. Once you become known as a competent maker of wine, you will be besieged, as I have been, by requests from those who want to assist in the entire operation. Thus, you may choose a reliable crew who, in time, will learn the procedure and give you efficient aid. Such a crew, having helped me for many years, are now so skilled that my own function in the several procedures is largely supervisory. And here I must emphasize the importance of engaging the children, as much as possible, in the cellar work as well as in the garden and the kitchen. Their participation in these basic familial activities, often sought by the more alert among them, will make children gradually aware of their own fundamental value; and, even more important, it will strengthen the intergenerational bond.

While the center of interest in the celebratory dinner is the wine, the state of being in the winemaker is a feeling of profound and ineffable satisfaction in the lively awareness that Bacchus is astride the barrel, his ancient throne, and all's well with the world. The dinner fare is designed to provoke thirst. The wise old peasants always served *baccala*, cod saturated with salt and sun-dried. Soaked in several changes of water for a day, it was broiled over glowing charcoal and given frequent bastings with a large sprig of rosemary dipped in a blend of wine vinegar and olive oil, aromatized with cloves of crushed garlic. I can still see the housewife, her glowing face reflecting the Bacchanalia, dipping the sprig in the blend and patting its vinegary drip on the *baccala*, accompanying each pat with gay, contrapuntal nods of the head. When done to a turn, the *baccala* was ceremoniously borne to the table with "Eat heartily, my children, you have done your work well."

As, indeed, they had. After a propitiatory toast to the wine god, their appetites given an additional edge by the pungent aroma of the broiling cod, they concentrated their attention on the feast: nothing more than *baccala*, the season's sweet fennel, loaves of heavy, well-baked brown bread, and liters of last year's wine. Of the new, they had brought to the table a large pitcher of the last thin flow and drip of the press, for it issues clean and clear and with a suggestion of sweetness. It was placed at the center of the table, a symbolic assurance of the year's indispensable supply of wine, and for everyone to taste and appraise.

As if in reverent praise of the housewife's culinary skill, the initial ingestion was in total silence. The *baccala* had its intended effect; after the first mouthful, while the grinding molars did their work, filled beakers, with beaded bubbles winking at the brim, were raised in reciprocal salutes and brought to the lips. Thereafter, the abundant drinking, whether required by the *baccala* or not, was routine and without ceremony. And when stomachs were full, and an irrepressible belch was greeted by "St. Anthony's blessing on you," and the men fired their pipes, the Apollonian-Dionysian mood was in its highest pitch. Francesco, with a wink at his young, voluptuous, tawny, full-lipped bride, Maria, sang a song suggested by the mood:

Quando di Maggio, le ciliege sono nere,
Che bel piacere, fare all'amor.
Lei sulla scala, e io di sotto che la reggo,
E tutto vedo, tutto cio che c'è lassú.

Do you get the drift? When in May cherries are ripe, Maria is high on the ladder picking them; and I, holding the ladder below, see all the glories of heaven. Of heaven? In those days peasant women wore ground-level skirts, but no panties. With that musical introduction to postprandial revels, you may imagine the rest. With Bacchus enthroned and Apollo in attendance, all was well with the world. Having thanked his crew and taken one last sip of the new wine, the Master went to bed. To sleep. Perchance, to dream about beakers full with beaded bubbles winking at the brim.

Having given an account of the sort of celebration that may follow the *svinatura*, I shall now describe the rackings that precede putting the wine in the oak barrel. Why oak rather than other hard wood? The reason is that the oak staves contribute necessary flavor and certain "extractives" to red wine, all of which add to the pleasing and subtle complexity of its taste and bouquet. Oak cooperage is universally used; but there is no agreement on how long the wine should be kept in the barrel, or on the time required by a red wine to extract the necessary virtues from the oak. However, all vintage wines are aged from two to four years in barrels of fifty- or sixty-gallon capacity before they are put in bottles. These are known in the industry as "small cooperage." The best are made of French limousin oak. In America, white oak from the forests of the South is extensively used. It is obvious, of course, that the smaller the barrel, the greater the exposure of the wine to the oak, and the less time required for the wine to extract its virtues. Thus, one year in a thirty-gallon barrel and two years in a fifty or sixty, would be long enough for the requirements of the amateur winemaker.

It has been my practice for the past twenty-five years to put the new wine in the barrel when it is brilliantly clear. To achieve this degree of clarity requires about six rackings, extending over two months, from the time the wine was drawn and put in carboys. Many winemakers put the new wine in the barrel immediately after it is drawn. I prefer my procedure for several reasons. There is a great deal of sediment, or lees, in the freshly drawn wine. Composed of dead yeast cells, ordinary field dirt that was on the grapes, tiny bits of stems, and other insoluble derivatives from the grape berry, the lees must be removed from the wine as soon as they drop to the bottom of the container, for prolonged contact with them affects the wine adversely. The removal is done by racking; and it's much easier to siphon from a carboy and rinse it afterward, than to siphon from the unwieldy barrel. Furthermore, in racking, you must avoid sucking up the sediment with the hose; for this reason the mouth of the hose is placed about an inch above the layer of sediment. Working with carboys, and being able to see precisely where the hose is placed, you can more effectively avoid drawing up the lees. A further justification of the procedure I advocate is is that, in the carboy, one can see when the sediment is deposited, and proceed immediately to the necessary racking. Another, and not the least advantage, is that because the wine is always brought to it clean, the precious aging barrel is never touched by the sedimentary filth deposited by the freshly drawn wine.

The racking may begin as soon as the deposit of sediment is clearly visible at the bottom of the carboys. Since it is unevenly distributed in the various carboys, there will be more sediment in some than others. That is to be expected. Where it is abundant and dense, it will settle within a day; and there will be more in the early than in the later racking. Remember, therefore, that when the line of demarcation between the wine and the lees is clearly visible, the racking must be done. When racked about six times, over a period of two months, the wine, to the naked eye, will be transparent. It may then be put in the barrel. There being now no further perceptible fermentation, bung the barrel airtight.

And here a word of caution. After the fermentation, air becomes the wine's enemy number one. Prolonged exposure to air causes oxidation, a "browning" of the wine; and it promotes the growth of aerobic vinegar bacteria. Therefore, the exposure must be kept at a minimum. While you are siphoning from one carboy into another, you can minimize exposure to the air by keeping the lower end of the hose submerged in the wine after the flow begins. Keep all containers filled to within a fraction of an inch of the base of the closure. Barrels lose by evaporation, through the wood, an amount of wine proportionate to their size. A fifty-gallon barrel loses about one bottle a month. In order to eliminate the consequent air space in the barrel, each barrel must be refilled every thirty days with wine reserved in jugs for that purpose. Lacking such reserve, use a good wine of the same variety. The process is known in the industry as topping. In these several ways, the wine's exposure to the air is kept at a minimum.

And this brings us, at long last, to the final operation: the bottling of the wine. That which is in the thirty-gallon barrel will be ready for the bottle after one year; that in the fifty, after two years. The bottling should be planned to coincide with the time when the new wine is ready for the barrel, so that as soon as the barrel is emptied, it can be washed and immediately refilled with the new wine. This avoids having an empty barrel on one's hands and all the woes that attend it, for the staves of empty barrels shrink, and the barrel itself may become infested with noxious bacteria. There are, of course, remedial measures against these nuisances, should they occur. But why gamble, when the procedure here suggested presents no difficulties, and assures one of tight, sound barrels in perpetuity?

In preparing for the bottling, have on hand the necessary clean bottles, corks that have been soaked in warm water for about ten hours, a rubber or plastic hose of sufficient length with an inner diameter of no more than a quarter inch, and a corking device that simultaneously compresses the cork and drives it into the neck of the bottle.

In siphoning the wine from the barrel into the bottle, the hose must be firmed to a solid rod several inches longer than the diameter of the barrel. (The storage barrel will be lying on its side, with the bung at the very center of the top.) Tie the intake end of the hose an inch above the lower end of the rod; tie it again at its upper end just above the bung hole of the barrel. Lower the rod slowly, straight down, into the barrel. When the lower end rests on the bottom, prevent it from moving by pressing a wad of cloth around the rod at the bung hole. Firming the intake end of the hose an inch above the lower end of the rod will prevent the hose from sucking up the sediment in the bottom of the barrel; tying it at the upper end will keep the hose firmed and straight along the rod. All of this must be done with care, so that during the siphoning process the rod with the hose attached remains immobile, for if the rod moves, ever so slightly, its lower end will roil the sediment and some of it will be sucked up into the bottle.

A crew of three is necessary to do the work properly and efficiently: one to do the siphoning, one to make sure each bottle is filled to the proper level, and the other to do the corking. Standard wine-bottle corks are about an inch and a quarter long. Some, used in bottling great vintages, are somewhat longer. In order to keep the air space in the bottle to a minimum, the bottle is filled to within a quarter-inch of the base of the cork. Since he who siphons cannot do this with precision, he passes the bottle to the checker who, provided with a small pitcher half-filled with wine, will add to or subtract from the bottle accordingly. He—or she—may, as one of my bibulous assistants prefers, occasionally sip the excess from the bottle. And why not! Then, in order to keep the cork moist and tight, the bottle is laid away on its side.

Red wine is initially aged in oak cooperage, but the definitive aging occurs in the bottle. Within limits, enologists can give an account of certain changes wine undergoes in the aging process; but beyond that, what occurs in the bottles remains Nature's secret, as much a secret as what has happened to a peach at full maturity to give it its unique flavor and fragrance. All one can say is that whatever was inherent in a given grape variety is fully realized after the grape has undergone all the procedures herein described, including aging in the bottle. This much man has established empirically; he has learned by decades of accumulated experience that the difference, noted on the palate and in the nose, between, let us say, a Cabernet wine when first bottled and the time that it is drunk ten years later, is as striking and perceptible as the difference between a gifted individual at sixteen years and at seventy, when he has attained his highest potential.

The analogy is most appropriate, for wine is a living organism, with a genetically determined life cycle. Wines that are "gifted" have a long life cycle, improve with age, and are few in number. Such are the great Cabernets, Pinots, Barolos, and several others. Lesser varieties, such as the Petite Sirah, Merlot, Gamay, are at their best when relatively young; and all undistinguished varieties, all generics, will not improve much after the first year. Indeed, they may be at their very best six months after fermentation. If sound when bottled, they may be kept longer; but they will not improve.

It is standard practice in wineries to filter wine before it is put in the bottle. This is done so that the consumer may never find a trace of sediment. The practice is regrettable and should be avoided. For filtering eviscerates the wine; that is, it removes from it all the microscopic solids, all the microorganisms whence, in the aging process, the wine derives its total character. It also decreases the density of the color. I very much doubt that a wine pressed from grapes of a superior variety, and therefore potentially great, will improve perceptibly in the bottle when thus purged. Frankly, I do not know with certainty. However, I do know that wines subjected to high-pressure filtration throw off no sediment in the bottle. How do I know? I have commercial wines, ten or more years old in my cellar, and not a trace of sediment.

And this means to me that the wine has been undergoing no change whatever in the bottle; for it is an inescapable fact of its nature, known to all experienced wine drinkers, particularly in Europe, that as a great wine ages, it excretes the consequent waste matter as sediment. The excretion proceeds slowly, imperceptibly, and becomes visible several years after the wine is bottled. Therefore, and assuming that the wine had not been afflicted with diarrhea, the connoisseur regards the sediment as proof that the wine is old and properly aged. He knows, also, that such wines must be decanted when served. Taken from the cellar where it has been lying on its side, a bottle of wine is stood upright until the sediment drops to the bottom; then the wine is poured very slowly, so as not to roil the sediment, into a decanter or another bottle.

Since the more sophisticated wine drinker in America is becoming aware of these regrettably little-known facts about wine, it is not surprising that Robert Mondavi, always intent on perfecting his cellar procedures, does not filter his great wines. In bottling some vintages, he notes, on the upper left corner of the label, *unfiltered.* I have some bottles of French Burgundy and Bordeaux twenty-three years old. The amount of sediment in them would probably frighten the test-tube boys who recommend filtering.

Such is the "recipe" for making red wines. I hope the

lady who asked me for it reads this book. White wines are made somewhat differently but in fundamentally the same way, for they, too, are the fermented juice of the grape with nothing added thereto and nothing subtracted therefrom. In the whites, the juice is extracted from the grape and fermented apart from the pomace; and the wine is not aged in the barrel for the reason that oak extractives are not desirable in white wine. What is desirable in it, when one uses one of the superior grape varieties, is the flavor and fragrance of the grape; and these are best attained by a slow and cool fermentation.

The procedure is as follows: Select the best white variety of vinifera grapes available. Crush them, do not remove the stems, and let them stand in an appropriate container for ten or fifteen hours. This much contact with the pomace is necessary for the must to assimilate the grape values inherent in the pulp and skins. Then extract the juice by pressing. Freshly crushed grapes yield their juice reluctantly, for they are slippery and tend to slither and squirt and slide in response to pressure in the press. The stems inhibit somewhat this perversity in the grape, and for this reason they are not removed.

Because of this difficulty in extracting the juice, and in order to recover all of it, the process is necessarily slow. Fill the press and apply the pressure until the flow of juice becomes a trickle. Then remove the crushed mass, loosen it thoroughly and repeat the process. If you don't run out of patience, press a third time. Do not hurry. Have a sip of the juice. Smell its incomparable fragrance. Whistle a merry tune. Recite a poem. Dance a jig. Dream on the gaiety you are storing up for the many tomorrows in this best of all possible worlds. This dalliance along the way will give each turn of the screw time to do its work.

When the pressing operation is completed, put the juice in a container large enough to hold all of it. (And here I would suggest that in your first venture you limit yourself to about thirty gallons.) Since you have pressed vinifera grapes, you may properly assume—and hope—that the sugar and acid are adequate. Prepare the yeast starter in two quarts of the juice in a gallon jug and immediately inoculate the rest with metabisulphite, using the proportion suggested for red wine (a hundred parts per million). Give the must a stir, and after several hours add the activated yeast starter. On the following day, transfer the must to carboys, fill them to about three-quarters of their capacity, plug them with a wad of absorbent cotton, and put them in the coolest place in the cellar. When the fermentation is well under way, it will generate a crown of bubbly foam. If that should moisten the cotton, replace it with a fresh wad.

The fermentation will proceed slowly, as it should if the cellar is cool, and be completed in about two weeks. Taste the wine at that time; and if there is no trace of sugar, rack it immediately, filling each carboy to within two inches of the top, and fitting it with a fermenting valve. Thereafter, the secondary fermentation will proceed slowly but perceptibly, causing tiny bubbles to rise and escape through the valve. This will continue for some time, the bubbles appearing at progressively longer intervals. When they are no longer visible, proceed with the racking. As was suggested earlier, in order to avoid sucking up the sediment, keep the intake end of the hose about an inch above the level of the sediment that you can see in the carboy. And remember to minimize the wine's contact with the air—a precaution that is especially important in making white wines—by keeping the outflow end of the hose submerged in the wine. After each carboy is thus racked, there will be some turbid wine left in it. Pour this remaining wine into a gallon jug; and as soon as the sediment settles, siphon off what is recoverable.

The fermentation is now completed, so the purpose of this and subsequent rackings is to clarify the wine. Accordingly, rack each carboy as soon as a layer of sediment becomes visible. And remember to keep the carboys filled to within a fraction of an inch of the corks, which may now be used as stoppers. Going into early winter, the wine should be brilliantly clear. It may then be bottled; or it may be left, sealed airtight, to age in the carboy. Within a year it will be ready to drink. If kept in the carboy, it may be transferred to gallon jugs as needed for the table. And when a jug is opened, the wine must be poured into five wine bottles and corked—unless you plan to use it all within a couple of days. These procedures are recommended in order to protect the wine from prolonged contact with the air.

Thus far we have proceeded on the assumption that vinifera grapes are used. If, however, one uses a labrusca variety, sugar has to be added to the must. This is easily done in the following way: Test the must for sugar with a Balling saccharometer. If the sugar content is 17 percent, in order to make wine of 12 percent alcohol by volume, add three and three quarter pounds of sugar for every ten gallons of must. If the percentage of sugar is 18, add two and three quarter pounds; if 19 percent, add one and three quarters; if 20, add three quarters of a pound. Use ordinary granulated sugar thoroughly dissolved in the necessary amount of juice. Stir it into the must, and proceed with the operations described for making wine with vinifera. Certain white varieites of labrusca yield a very fine wine, so do not hesitate to use it—especially if you enjoy the smell of the den of a fox.

This muted praise of labrusca grapes, the species indigenous to our land, concludes my account of how wine is made. You have read with care, followed all the instructions; and now that we are once again in the season of mists and mellow fruitfulness, happy with the result of your first effort, ready to undertake the second in full confidence and with added zest, I welcome you as a novitiate into the order of Wise Old Peasants, of which I am privileged to be President. In celebration thereof, have a bibulous dinner party. And if by chance there is in your lineage some abstemious sourpuss—is that redundant?—who has followed your cellar work with despairing shakes of the head, enthrone that person at the head of the table. Serve a dish appropriate to the Order you have been invited to join: pig trotters, pig tails, and navy or other white beans.

Braise the tails and trotters—split lengthwise—in a skillet drenched with a good olive oil. Do it slowly and until they are nicely browned. Meanwhile simmer the beans in water enriched with a tablespoon of granular beef or chicken bouillon until they are half cooked. Remove the browned tails and trotters with a slotted spoon from the skillet, and prepare therein the sauce. Mince and sauté a medium-size onion—the proportions are for six hearty eaters—a rib of celery, half a carrot, and two tablespoons of finely diced fat and lean salt pork. Do not burn or brown. When these appear to be done enough, add three cloves of garlic coarsely chopped. Follow these with a heaping table-spoon of minced parsley and a level one of thyme. Deglaze with a cup of white wine. Combine a cup of beef broth or bouillon and one third of a cup of pure tomato sauce enliv-ened with a dash or two of Tabasco sauce. Stir in half a teaspoon of arrowroot for thickening. Pour this mixture into the skillet and stir and simmer it for a few minutes. The sauce should be abundant and quite fluid. Use what-ever salt and pepper you desire.

Arrange the tails and trotters in a Dutch oven or its equivalent. Sprinkle them with salt and pepper and drown the critters in the savory sauce. Bake, covered, in an oven preheated to three hundred fifty degrees, until nearly done —about two hours. Test them from time to time with a fork and add whatever wine and broth are necessary to keep them drowned. When your test indicates that the toughies—is there such a word?—are getting tender, spread the drained and partly cooked beans over them. Then, with a fork, raise trotters and tails just enough to let some of the beans slip under them and into the sauce. Hav-ing effected this culinary marriage ceremony, return the twain to the oven to simmer together for about thirty min-utes, or until such time as the meat falls from the bone and the beans are tender. Serve the hearty peasant dish fear-lessly—only relatively rich peasants can afford it—and proceed with the bibulous dinner. You are celebrating your first anniversary as an amateur winemaker of distinction, along with your induction into the Order of Wise Old Peasants.

Glowing with unabashed self-satisfaction, raise your glass, turn toward the abstemious sourpuss at the head of the table, and propose a toast: Some years ago in a restaurant in Florence, two abstemious Italian artists, Monello and Vellani-Marchi, were persuaded to drink a glass of Lambrusco. Not bad, said the one to the other. Not bad at all, said the other to the one. And thereafter, with no further urging, they drained several glasses. After lunch they left the restaurant, arm in arm, muttering to each other: "What fools we have been to have remained abstemious for these many years." Their conversion was effected by Paolo Monelli, an irresistibly persuasive Italian writer on gastronomy. And to him we drink this toast: Long may he live, to lead men out of their folly.

The Mystique of Wine

"In wine talk and wine tasting, there is an enormous amount of humbug and a great deal of pretense." I have forgotten who made this statement; but accept it as a fact and be wary of connoisseurs, especially the scribbling sort, whose attitude toward wine is one of awesome veneration, and who have conferred upon it a mythical status. Such solemnity is utterly ridiculous; and not infrequently it is a self-serving posture designed to set the connoisseur apart from the ordinary wine-drinker who takes his wine in stride, as he takes his bread. It is understandable and most appropriate that such serious writers as Hemingway and Steinbeck should pay their respects to wine by referring to it as "one of the most beautiful things in life," and as the "Holy Blood of the grape." Some such metaphor would do justice to certain others of Nature's gifts intended for the palate and the stomach.

But note some of the solemn absurdities recorded by the scribblers. It has been alleged that a certain wine was so venerable that, to do it justice, an entire gourmet dinner had to be built around it; that a certain other was such an elixir that it had to be taken in reverent sips from a silver chalice; that a great Chablis is the only appropriate wine to drink with oysters. How can anyone who has not taken leave of his wits fail to laugh at such pretensions! And how about you? Are you not ashamed, humbled, humiliated, for having floated fried oysters to your stomach on hearty draughts of the most ordinary table wine? Certainly not! Possibly, when, as a wine drinker you were still in your salad days, you might have been humbled by such a reproach; but now that you are a wise old peasant with purpled feet and purple-stained mouth, you are unimpressed. And properly so.

For now you understand that bread and wine are twins; that either without the other is but half itself. You are so sensibly aware of this gastronomic truth that, even if you were pinned to the wall, you could not honestly say which is more important on a dinner table blessed with plenty of both. You know, also, that bread and wine vary in quality. Furthermore, with your knowledge of grape species, and as a competent winemaker, you can account for the degrees of excellence in wine, a competence and a knowledge ordinary wine scribblers are not likely to have. So, who is a connoisseur?

A good question. If the word refers to one who can distinguish a very good from an indifferent wine, then there are millions of wine drinkers who qualify as connoisseurs. But the word means more than that, for it is descriptive of a person with "informed and astute discrimination," especially concerning the arts and matters of taste. How many are thus endowed? By definition, very few. In the realm of food and wine, what feats of informed and astute discrimination establish the connoisseur's authority?

Here the scribblers record some amazing instances. It has been alleged that a French connoisseur of food could tell whether a trout had been caught upstream or downstream from a certain bridge on the Seine, and name every ingredient of the sauce in which it was cooked. Not at all a shabby performance! And even less so that of certain connoisseurs of wine who, after a sniff and a sip of a given wine, could deduce its quality, variety, age, and place of origin. And again: Two such connoisseurs, competing for supremacy, drew wine from a barrel and proceeded to judgment. The one identified it, gave its age, place of origin, and pronounced it perfect but for a slight defect: There was a trace of metal in it. The other agreed; but he detected a further blemish: The wine had a ropy aftertaste. And he emerged the victor, for when the barrel was emptied, a key was found in its bottom. And attached to it was a length of household twine.

Another feat of incredibly difficult discriminatory judgment was as follows: An unusually endowed connoisseur, given a glass of wine, was asked to name what it reminded him of. After a sniff and a sip he said: "Urine." Then, as if to underscore the sensitivity of his nose and palate, he added: "Yes! The urine of a duchess." Since one cannot identify that which he has not previously known, one wonders how often he had sniffed the waste expelled from the bladder of—was it his Last Duchess?

Such improbable feats as here recorded are drawn from the mystique, the mythology of wine. And so are certain words and phrases which are intended to be descriptive of wines, but which tend to mystify the ordinary wine drinker: imperious, balanced, flinty, foxy, having a consoling feminine aftertaste, velvety, harmonious, fruity, resembling bottled sunshine. It's no wonder that wine drinkers in America, intent on learning about wine, tend to approach it with regrettable diffidence. Since they cannot discern such subtleties in it, they either parrot the glib connoisseurs or conclude that they themselves lack the sensitivity of nose and palate necessary to appreciate wine's sublime virtues.

And that attitude, I say, is regrettable; anyone with an unstuffed nose and a normal palate and some experience in drinking wine, though not able to give them a name, can appreciate its sublime virtues. This I have proved to my complete satisfaction. On many occasions I have given such men and women a glass of great and one of an ordinary wine, without telling them which was which; and invariably they have raved about the one and dismissed the other with a shrug of the shoulders. These were intelligent, though not necessarily learned, and unbiased individuals eager to learn more about wine. On the other hand, an affluent disciple of the mystique coterie, and therefore something of a snob, proclaimed that only French wines were fit to drink; and that a certain California Cabernet was hogwash. In a blind tasting of two very good French and two California Cabernets, he chose the hogwash. Perhaps his palate prevailed over his bias.

So much for humbug, pretense, and misplaced veneration in wine talk and wine tasting. I want now to examine what measure of truth there is in the statement that after a sniff and a sip, a connoisseur can deduce the quality, variety, age, and place of origin of a given wine. Can it be done? Taking the statement as it stands, the answer is no. Properly qualified, the answer is yes. The wine to be thus identified must have an ascertainable identity; and the governing logic of such a test requires that the connoisseur should have had antecedent knowledge of it. For how can one identify that which he has not previously known? A further fact to consider in this context is that only a precious few wines have an identifiable character. The ordinary wines of America and Europe, the least expensive or moderately priced varietals, in jugs or in bottles, are generally made from grapes grown in different vineyards and so standardized in production that they have no identity, no individuality. For these reasons, such wines cannot be identified by anyone.

Bearing these qualifications in mind, let us give the connoisseur a glass of genuine Cabernet, one of equally genuine Pinot Noir and a third glass of genuine Zinfandel. Will he be able to identify the Cabernet and the Pinot? Most certainly, provided he has had considerable previous sensory knowledge of those two varieties; and most certainly not if he lacked such knowledge. Such a test would be relatively simple for a qualified judge. More difficult would be one that required him to give the age of the two wines; but he could do it, provided that some time in the past he had tasted the two vintages, noted the date, and had a good taste memory. It would be extremely difficult, if not impossible, if he were required to do what a wine snob bet he could do at a dinner party recorded in Roald Dahl's short story, "Taste."

The host announced that the dinner wine was a great vintage Bordeaux. The bottle had been opened an hour ago so that the bouquet, long imprisoned in the bottle, might have time to come alive before the wine was poured into the tulip-shaped glasses on the table. The maid would fetch the wine from the pantry at the proper time. The guest, a glib, self-appointed connoisseur of Bordeaux wines, bet that he could identify it. The terms of the wager were set, the bottle, enfolded in a linen napkin, was brought to the table, and the mystery wine was poured, each glass half full. In serving great vintages especially, that is the proper amount, for before taking the first sip, one swishes the wine in the glass in order to admire its color and note the so-called tears, the wine's viscosity and oiliness, which fall slowly down the side of the glass after the rotating swish. The more or less ceremonial gesture also aids the bouquet's rise to the expectant nostrils.

Having performed this preliminary maneuver, the guest sniffed the wine and took a first sip. What he proposed to do would severely tax the resources of the most accomplished connoisseur, for in Bordeaux there are a dozen or so top wineries, known in the trade as *chateaux*, as well as many lesser ones. Had he tasted wines from all of them, including the one on the table? Did he have the necessary taste and olfactory memory to distinguish the one on the table from all the rest? As he proceeded in his analysis, he displayed an enormous amount of book knowledge of Bordeaux wines. That is, he knew the recorded characteristics of the various *chateaux:* Margaux, Haut-Brion, Lafitte, and the rest. He had in mind, also, words and phrases used by competent connoisseurs to describe the most famous *chateaux*. Thus armed, he began his dazzling performance.

Cautiously sniffing and sipping, he eliminated the *chateaux* in the St. Émilion and Graves districts, giving his reasons for the elimination. Therefore, the wine must be from the Médoc. He sniffed and sipped once more, closed his eyes, pondered, and was certain. Sniffing victory, he eliminated Margaux and Pauillac. Why? The wine to be identified lacked the violent bouquet of the one and the imperious character of the other. Furthermore, it had a consoling, feminine aftertaste. Once again he searched his memory and remembered that such consoling femininity was found only in the wines of the St. Julien commune. He knew now that he was on target; and the host began to fear that he would lose the wager. But since there were several *chateaux* in that district, the guest might not hit upon the right one. However, methodically stating his reasons with uncanny accuracy—wine dilettantes have such a store of book knowledge of wine!—the guest eliminated all but two: Chateau Talbot and Chateau Branaire-Ducru, 1934. Another sniff, another sip, another concentrated effort to remember, and he ruled out Talbot. And the host congratulated the winner.

The winner? Just a moment, mine host! While the guest was crowing modestly and moaning over the difficulty of his performance, the maid brought him his spectacles. He had left them in the pantry after he had examined the bottle of wine.

And this concludes the account of pretense and humbuggery in wine scribblings and wine tasting. It seemed to me an appropriate conclusion to the pleasure of advising the amateur winemaker, for it is fitting that you should know something about the nontechnical wine "literature" in which certain absurdities are recorded; know within what limits one may qualify as a wine connoisseur; and know that to identify a given vintage wine—its age and place of origin—in a line-up of wines, one must have had a previous sensory experience of it. The cheating by the guest in the story simply underscores the extreme difficulty, if not the impossibility, implicit in doing what he pretended to do, as the example I am about to give underscores the ease with which such an identification may be made in a totally different set of circumstances, by the ordinary wine drinker.

I have in my cellar two Cabernets. The grapes for the one came from the Napa Valley and for the other, from the Santa Clara Valley. The one is two years older than the other; and though of equal excellence, they are perceptibly different. People who have been drinking wine regularly for several years, having sniffed and tasted them until they were certain that they knew each one, given a blind test immediately thereafter, had no difficulty whatever in identifying them. Could they identify them in a line-up of Cabernets two or three years later? Possibly, if they had the necessary taste memory. I, myself, when the younger wine was some years older, and the difference between them was more subtle, could not easily distinguish one from the other. And this simply means that when the difference between two wines is not substantial, only an experienced wine drinker with a very sensitive nose and palate can discern that difference.

In conclusion, let us abide by certain fundamentals:

Bread and wine of excellent quality are complementary on the dinner table; the one strengthens the heart, the other makes it gay. Let us respect them for what each does and strive to have the best of both. There are indifferent wines, good wines, superior wines. And the experienced wine drinker who can discern the degrees of excellence in wine, and never fails to recognize a good wine, is the genuine connoisseur—with no apologies to the esoteric fraternity. William James once said that the social value of the college-bred person consists in his knowing a good man when he meets one. Similarly, a wine connoisseur is one who knows a good wine when he drinks one.

FIVE

Epilogue

"THE curfew tolls the knell of parting day." My work is done. The time is April, 1983, the "cruellest month," according to the poet of the *Waste Land.* I have never found it so! And the April of this year is especially dear to me. For I have begun the eightieth year of my life and the seventieth year of my residence in America. And by a happy coincidence, in a few days I shall deliver the manuscript of this, my eighth book, to my editor.

The "cruellest" month? Not so for me! This morning, while the birds were chirping and twittering their epithalamia, and I was humming "Whan that Aprill with his shoures soote . . ." I pressed the seed for a second row of peas into the fertile soil. The ones in the first row, sown in mid-February, were about to begin their ascent up the supporting poles. Then I fed each of my artichoke plants a handful of urea. How they love that white, crystalline compound, found in mammalian urine! But then—there is no accounting for the vagaries of taste.

My next labor was more muscular, the sort that makes one sweat, a corrective for prolonged sitting at one's desk. Remember what Emerson said about the therapeutic virtue of such labor. I prepared the soil for sowing pole beans later in the month. I spread manure over the area and incorporated it into the ground by spading. Then I raked the spaded area to achieve a neat, even surface, smoothed the hillocks, removed stones and other rubble. And when

all this was done, I mopped my brow, put away my garden tools, and stood for a moment to survey what I had done and to make sure that it was properly done. It was; and I was happy.

I took another look at the artichoke plants. The fruit-bearing stem was beginning to rise from the root crown. How many laterals would it have? Would each bear an artichoke of edible size? Had the roots yet begun to assimilate the urea? I was not impatient, just curious, wanting to know the precise mechanism by which roots ingest such putrid stuff as manure and urea, and transform it into nutrients that give the end products of plants their total character. Despairing that I would never know such secrets of Nature, I simply told the plants to get on with it, so that I might have fried artichoke hearts by the middle of May.

It was midday now and I was hungry. What should I eat? Leeks and chard and witloof chicory and Savoy cabbage had survived the winter. Why not a frittata made with a combination of the first two? Excellent idea! With a muttered farewell to the kitchen garden, I rushed into the house and took a shower. Then I went to the cellar to fetch a bottle of the Holy Blood of the grape, vintage Cabernet, 1971, pressed from perfect grapes sent to me from the Napa Valley. While in the cellar, it being the time to top the barrels, I added a bottle to each of the two sixty-gallon casks and a half bottle to the one of thirty-gallon capacity. With that bit of pleasant cellar work done, I returned to the kitchen, pulled the cork from the bottle, poured myself half a glass and drank it quickly in order to restore to the body the fluid I had lost as sweat; quickly, I say, for in ministering to the needs of the body, there are some things that must not be postponed.

The wine was such that only appropriate metaphors can suggest its total character: authoritative, masculine, imperious, sacramental. It reminded me of what Dante meant when he said of a great wine: "Behold what happens when the heat of the sun transforms the humor that flows in the vine." I knew, when I did my cellar work on the perfect grapes, that the wine would be great; and the promise of greatness was there. But it would take another five years in the bottle to achieve it.

When I had made the frittata, the lost fluid in my body now restored, I, happy as the grass is green, sat down to enjoy my well-earned lunch. The indispensable bread had been baked the day before. Only one thing was lacking to extract from the moment its full measure of joy—my wife. She and I always klink glasses by way of grace when we sit down to dinner. She was at her club assisting in the final arrangements for its annual arts and crafts fair. So before taking the ritual first sip of wine, I held my glass up to her image, winked, brought to glass to my lips, set it down, and attacked the frittata.

When I had tended to my belly very carefully and very studiously, I lay down for half an hour so that no muscular activity might disturb the gastric juices as they attacked the ingested nutrients. And now restored, refreshed, spiritual-ized, I am back at my desk. Now that you have seen me at work in the garden, the kitchen, and the cellar, you will know that I do precisely what I have urged you to do in this, my culinary testament, my eighth book, completed in April, the month of my nativity, the month of showers, "of which vertu engendered is the flour."

Therefore, reconsider the values by which you want to live, grow your own, cook your own, make your own wine. Live in harmony with Nature. And may you find the promised fatness that inheres in the lean and therefore happy years.

Scotland Street